Above all, always and everywhere, that which brings the fundamental forces into harmony, that which leads all beings toward unity, is called *love*.

What is the work of love toward each other that can support the search for unity within ourselves? What can we realistically give each other that helps us be *given to*—by what religion calls God, by what philosophy calls Reality, and by what wisdom calls the Self?

This book is intended to open this question in relation to the actual difficulties we all face in working at love—problems of communication, trust, the pressures of time, and the demands of the bewildering, dramatically changing world in which we all must search for each other and for ourselves.

QUANTITY SALES

Most Dell books are available at special quantity discounts when purchased in bulk by corporations, organizations, or groups. Special imprints, messages, and excerpts can be produced to meet your needs. For more information, write to: Dell Publishing, 1540 Broadway, New York, NY 10036. Attention: Director, Special Markets.

INDIVIDUAL SALES

Are there any Dell books you want but cannot find in your local stores? If so, you can order them directly from us. You can get any Dell book currently in print. For a complete up-to-date listing of our books and information on how to order, write to: Dell Readers Service, Box DR, 1540 Broadway, New York, NY 10036.

A Little Book on
LOVE

Jacob Needleman

A DELL BOOK

Published by
Dell Publishing
a division of
Bantam Doubleday Dell Publishing Group, Inc.
1540 Broadway
New York, New York 10036

ISBN: 0-440-22666-X

Reprinted by arrangement with Currency Books, a division of Doubleday

Printed in the United States of America

Published simultaneously in Canada

November 1998

10 9 8 7 6 5 4 3 2 1

OPM

For my wife

CONTENTS

Part 1   THE WORK OF LOVE   1

Chapter One   Love and Wisdom   3

Chapter Two   The Two Loves   23

Chapter Three   Communication   46

Chapter Four   Why do We Quarrel?   60

Chapter Five   Trust   74

Chapter Six   Time   89

Chapter Seven   Money, Work, Sex, Power,

                 Beauty . . . Life Itself   99

CONTENTS

Part 2   THE WISDOM OF LOVE   115

Chapter Eight   Intentional Love   117

Chapter Nine   Ethics as Love   128

Chapter Ten   Two Poets: Rumi and Rilke   144

Chapter Eleven   Impersonal Love   156

Chapter Twelve   The Practice of Love   169

Conclusion in The Form of a Question   179

For Further Reading   193

A Little Book on
LOVE

Part 1

THE WORK OF LOVE

Chapter One

LOVE AND WISDOM

Who has not been humbled by love, by its joys and its sorrows? How many of us try again and again to lay hold of what love seems to promise, only to be thrown back in fear or confusion or pain? How many give up and sadly accept to live outside the drama of love?

Whatever the meaning of our lives may be, it has to involve love. But what kind of love? Almost all the myths and legends and stories that teach us about love deal with the force that brings us together, in passion. And then—leads us into what?

Among the world's most profound love stories, there is one that is rarely noticed alongside the blazing tales of passion that reach us from the ancient and medieval worlds. In the legend of Philemon and Baucis, we find no bewitched love potion of the kind that carries Tristan and Isolde to their consummation in death, no heart-wrenching journey to the kingdom of Hades, where Orpheus, with one impatient glance, loses his Eurydice for all eternity.

Like a faint star which we can see only with new eyes, the myth of Philemon and Baucis gives a subtle light that suggests another kind of reality, another kind of love. And who can deny that our world is starved for a new understanding of love, of what it means to live together and work at love and not give up? That is the inquiry that the myth can start in us.

Our only source of the story is the great Roman chronicler of love and transformation, Ovid.* Ovid's speaker is Lelex, "ripe in years and wisdom."

---

* *The Metamorphoses* of Ovid, trans. by Mary M. Innes, Harmondsworth, Middlesex, England: Penguin Books, Ltd., 1955, 1973, Book III, 615–725, pp. 195–98.

"In the hill country of Phrygia," he begins, "there is an oak, growing close beside a linden tree, and a low wall surrounds them both. I have seen the spot myself. . . ."

Close by, it seems, where once there was habitable land and a thriving village, there is now only a lake of stagnant water haunted by marsh birds. Jupiter, lord of gods and men, once visited this land with his companion, Mercury. Disguised as mortals, they wandered from house to house to see who would be willing to receive them and offer them a place to rest and take nourishment.

"The two gods went to a thousand homes and found a thousand doors bolted and barred against them." The gods do not force themselves upon us; they enter only where the door is opened for them.

Only one house takes them in—"a humble dwelling roofed with thatch and reeds from the marsh." They are welcomed by a good-hearted old woman, Baucis, and her husband, Philemon. The tale says that Baucis and Philemon are of the same age, that they had been married in that cottage in their youth, and had "grown gray in it together."

Everything in the ancient stories echoes its meanings on many levels. Who pays attention now to the symbol of the married couple living together from youth to old age? What kind of love is represented here? And why is it they, and they alone, who allow the gods into their home?

Baucis and Philemon are poor, but the tale does not simply mention their poverty; it tells us how they regarded it. "They confessed their poverty." They saw their poverty for what it was, without hiding it from themselves. Through this acceptance "they eased the hardship of their lot." Certainly it is not only physical poverty that is spoken of in the ancient language of myth.

"It made no difference in that house whether you asked for master or servant—the two of them were the entire household: the same people gave the orders and carried them out." Why put it this way?

The "heaven dwellers" are welcomed in and must stoop to pass through the low doorway. Simple wooden chairs are offered them and a fire is fed with leaves and dried bark to warm them. After much bustling activity and hospitable talk, a meal of vegetables, cheese, berries, and carefully roasted eggs is set out in rude clay dishes, and wine "of no great age" is passed around.

"As the dinner went on, the old man and

woman saw that the flagon, as often as it was emptied, refilled itself of its own accord." Seeing this, Baucis and Philemon recognize the true nature of their guests and are filled with awe and fear. Timidly stretching out their hands in prayer, they beg the gods' indulgence for a poor meal. They have a single goose which they have kept as a kind of guardian of their small plot of land, but seeing now who their visitors are, they make ready to kill the bird. The goose runs from them and takes refuge with the gods, who declare that it should not be killed. It is not the goose who must be destroyed, say the gods, but the people of this place who refused to receive them. Only Baucis and Philemon are to be spared. They are asked to leave their poor house and ascend a steep mountain with the gods as their guides and companions. "The two old people both did as they were told and, leaning on their sticks, struggled up the long slope."

Baucis and Philemon are led to a "higher level" and now see nothing but water where once there was a land full of living people. What kind of gods are these? Are we being given a picture of divine spite and vengeance—or is something deeper at issue here, involving the purpose of human life itself and the fateful consequences of man's unwillingness to accept this purpose—as in the Old Testament legend of Noah and the Flood?

The only structure that remains amid all the desolation is the house in which Baucis and Philemon had spent their lives together—*serving each other* (where there was neither "master nor servant"). And now they are astonished to see that their poor hut has been transformed into a temple of the gods. "As they wept for the fate of their people, their old cottage, which had been small, even for two, was changed into a temple; marble columns took the place of its wooden supports, the thatch grew yellow, till the roof seemed to be made of gold, the doors appeared magnificently adorned with carvings, and marble paved the earthen floor."

Then Jupiter, son of Saturn, speaks to them in majestic tones and offers to grant whatever they ask from him. The tale gives us the picture of the old man and woman stepping back and consulting with each other in whispered voices. What is it they wish from the lord of the heavens?

"We ask to be your priests, to serve your shrine; and since we have lived in happy companionship all our lives, we pray that death may carry

us off together at the same instant. . . ." Their
prayer is granted. For the rest of their lives, they
live as the priests of Jupiter in the sacred space of
the temple.

Now Ovid tells us of the transformation that
is the mysterious culmination of the story. One
day, bowed down with the weight of years, they are
standing on the steps of the temple, talking of all
that has happened there. Suddenly Baucis sees
Philemon beginning to put forth leaves and
Philemon sees the same happening to his wife.
"When the tree-tops were already growing over
their two faces, they exchanged their last words
while they could and cried simultaneously: 'Good-
bye, my dear one!' As they spoke the bark grew over
and concealed their lips. The Bithynian peasant
still points out the trees growing there side by side,
trees that were once two bodies."

Almost everyone who has recounted this tale in
modern times, such as Bulfinch or Edith Hamilton,
stops there and follows Ovid no further. And at
this point the image of the two lovers transformed
into intertwined trees has at best a bittersweet flavor, and may seem grotesque even as a symbol—
for a symbol must speak truly at all levels, includ-

ing the literal level. A symbol has to be concretely true, true of the life we see and hear and touch as well as being true of the invisible life we search for within ourselves. So, perhaps, something is not quite right here. Why no "happily ever after"? Have the two lovers not actually died, after all? Does the story give us no hope of something beyond what we see and hear and touch right before our eyes?

This is a strange fairy tale. And yet, it sounds something entirely new about love. Most fairy tales have their mystery—their navel, as it were—right in the middle. This tale has its mystery at the end. What kind of love can we search for in our work of living together? What do we serve in each other? And to what do we need to open ourselves in each other and from the realms above and within ourselves, the "realms of the gods"?

What are these trees that intertwine, and that never die? And, finally, why does the tale end, not as the modern narrators inform us, but with the speaker, Lelex, offering the following: "This tale was told me by responsible old men, who had nothing to gain by deceiving me. Indeed, I myself have seen the wreaths hanging on the branches, and have hung up fresh ones, saying:

" 'Whom the gods love are gods themselves, and those who have worshiped should be worshiped too.' "

The story thus ends by pointing to the real meaning of the transformation of the two lovers. When the ancient wisdom speaks of mortals becoming gods, it is telling us about the birth of a new and higher self, or soul, within ourselves. It is this inner birth that has been served by the marriage of Philemon and Baucis.

The Teachings of Wisdom

But now we have our own experience to consult, our own encounters with another god, the god of love, who is known in heaven and earth for the trouble and distress that love brings alongside its joy and passion. Amid everything that our culture suggests to us about love, is there a new understanding of what it means to *hold* love, to sustain love, so that it serves as more than a blazing but transient glimpse of happiness; so that it supports the journey toward the birth within ourselves of a new and more authentic humanity?

This understanding of love does exist. It comes from ancient worlds and it is implicit in the teachings of wisdom that have been handed down since time immemorial. But like a distant star itself, this view of love is not easily seen amid civilization's manufactured lights which so often blind us to the presence of the stars . . . and the gods.

What, exactly, do we mean when we speak of "the teachings of wisdom"? This phrase will appear again and again as a source of guidance as we reflect on the question of love. Does there in fact exist a body of knowledge that comes from the ancient worlds and that deserves the name of wisdom?

Here we are squarely in front of the invitation to open our doors to the gods. The question confronts us in this way: How to regard the ideas about human nature and the universal world that lie at the heart of the great spiritual teachings and philosophies of the world? And what kind of struggle is needed for us to live our lives according to these teachings?

It is not difficult to identify some of the doctrines that lie at the heart of mankind's spiritual traditions. As modernity brings the peoples of the world closer and closer together, it is now possible to discern the outlines of a fundamental vision that over the millennia has been adapted to every culture within the human family. What remains difficult, however, is to understand why this vision has so little influence on the way men and women actually conduct their lives.

The hidden aspect of the "great wisdom" is not so much a matter of which ideas are comprised by it as it is the nature of the difficulty in putting these ideas into practice. To grasp this point is to understand in a new way what kind of help people need from each other and can give to each other. It is this dimension of love that the present book seeks to uncover.

But what, to begin with, are the elements of this ancient universal teaching that lies at the root of the world's religions and spiritual philosophies? What does it tell us about human nature and the world we must live in? This vision embraces an immense body of ideas about the whole of human life and the world of nature. What follows is a sketch of one or two central components of this vision.

Human beings, we are told, carry within themselves a very great possibility and, corresponding to this possibility, a great obligation. We have the possibility of opening ourselves to a quality of life and consciousness that transcends anything we ordinarily experience as happiness or knowledge or meaning. When this quality of conscious life becomes active in us, we begin to understand for ourselves, down deep in our being, what human life is meant to serve. We discover, according to these teachings, that the power to think clearly, to see the connectedness of things, is a function of the action of this conscious life. We discover that the capacity to love in a nonegoistic way also flows from this same consciousness.

This teaching about the inner world lies at the heart of the ideas and moral systems of the world's religions. For many of us in the modern era, however, our knowledge about religion came to us without any reference to the idea of the inner world and the need to develop our access to a new and higher quality of consciousness within ourselves. Judaism and Christianity, as most of us know them, come to us mainly as doctrine, with little indication of the practical steps that must be taken in order to live according to the doctrine and to verify its truth alongside the worldview of modern science.*

Along with this notion of the inner world and the necessity of opening to the conscious forces that lie within us, the religious and spiritual teachings of the world rest upon a remarkably comprehensive vision of the outer world as well. Far from contradicting the discoveries of science, this vision of the cosmic scheme seems to be confirmed by the direction that our science is now taking as it reveals to us a universe not only unimaginably vast, but unimaginably alive and dynamic, constantly giving birth to worlds upon worlds with a fecundity and integrity that humbles all our attempts at theoretical explanation.

According to this ancient vision, the universe has far more in it than the kind of entities that modern science can see or infer. There are layers of

* As a rule, we are not given the means to translate the mythic language of the old religions into a discourse that corresponds to the mindset of modernity. This, too, is a result of being acquainted with the doctrines of religion without any hint that these doctrines or ideas cannot ultimately be separated from the practical method that guides the individual's actual experience.

laws and influences that enclose us as a great organism "encloses" the cells and tissues within it, and that support or oppose us in ways we cannot perceive with the senses. This "vertical" structure of the cosmos is spoken of mythically in all cultures: in the angels and devils of the Semitic religions, in the gods of ancient Egypt and Greece, in the thousands and millions of Hindu deities and demons, in the cosmic protectors and destroyers of Buddhism, in the spirit forces in Native American, African, and other teachings of the world's peoples. In philosophical language, this vertical cosmos may be characterized, as was done by Plato in the Greek world or by Maimonides in the world of medieval Judaism, as a universe of levels of consciousness and will, a universe populated by intermediate levels between mankind and the Absolute God.

But whether the language is mythic, symbolic, or philosophical, the idea is the same: mankind is enmeshed in a vast living cosmos containing levels of mind and purpose that far exceed what we normally experience as our own capacity of thought and will. Moreover, *this whole cosmic order is reflected within the human psyche.* The vertical structure of the inner world is as immense as the vertical structure of the universe itself. *We are unknown to ourselves.* We live not only, as modern science tells us, in a tiny corner of the universe of matter; we live in a tiny constricted corner of our own inner universe as well. The teachings of the great traditions thus complement the findings of modern science and show us mankind as an intersection between two infinities—each one beckoning to us, but both together comprising the role that mankind is meant to occupy in the whole scheme of things.

We are meant to live in two infinities at once—one leading us outward toward action in the world around us; the other calling us to open ourselves to the world within us. All the teachings agree: our capacity to live meaningfully, wisely, and compassionately depends entirely on our openness to the higher reaches of the inner world.

All these ideas and many others related to them have begun to enter our culture in response to a growing need not only among younger people, but among men and women of all ages and walks of life. Involvement in such teachings and practices as Buddhism, Jewish and Christian mysticism, Sufism and Hinduism, as well as Native American and African spiritual traditions, to name only a few, is no longer confined to a so-called "new age" fringe. The search for transcendence and for inner development now calls to many of the most responsible and established members of our culture in the world of business, science, and the arts. In this sense, we are beginning to be what to some extent we were when our country was founded: a nation of seekers.

But having been drawn to modern expressions of the universal spiritual tradition, men and women must conduct their day-to-day lives in a world governed by forces that may be implacably opposed to the process of inner awakening. With each passing year, the tensions and anxieties of modern life seem to intensify, the confusion of purpose spreads, the foundations of family life, meaningful work, and social identity seem more and more endangered and more and more enmeshed in the paranoia and divisiveness of political shrillness and suspicion. Everywhere money factors, with all their complicatedness and unconscious egoism, influence what were once sacred, intimate islands of human concern: living and dying, the education of children, and, of course, love. More and more, modern life is a life of conflict and battles—at work, at home, and among the thousands of associations and groups throughout our country and our culture. Modern technology, with the blood of commerce and busyness running through every fiber and silicon chip, meets us decisively at all the crossroads of our minds and hearts to the point that its influence is no longer limited to its physical presence everywhere. In many cases, the new technologies have actually taken the place of philosophy and religion in determining the conduct of our lives. More often than we may realize, the instruments have become the masters, telling us what we must do in our lives and why.

All the great spiritual traditions speak of the world's opposition to the inner life. In Christianity it was called the world of the "flesh," in Buddhism it is the "wheel of *samsara*," in the spiritual philosophies of ancient Greece it is the life of the "masses." The names are legion, but the idea is the same: the general process of civilization opposes inner growth. The general process of human life is based on material values, spiritual illusions, agitation, and innumerable forms by which human beings are drawn into identifying themselves with the animal or mechanical aspects of the self. Along with that error, they are drawn into the hidden assumption that the happiness or well-being of one's own self or of those nearest to one constitutes the greatest good, a deeply rooted assumption that breeds hatred, injustice, violence, and war, often intensified by moral or religious self-righteousness. Under the sway of these influences, mankind loses the possibility of understanding its genuine and fundamental obligation, which, as all the teachings agree, is to place oneself at the service of the universal forces of love and consciousness both within the self and at the foundation of the universe. Mankind is built for that service—that love. It is not oversimplifying to characterize all the spiritual traditions as saying that all human misery results from ignorance of or resistance to this intrinsic obligation, and that all authentic human happiness and well-being, as well as all authentic moral action, result from opening to the higher forces within and above the individual self.

But each era, each civilization has its own particular coloration, and the obstacles to inner growth take different forms, however similar they are under the surface. Always and everywhere, the difficulties standing in the seeker's way are more subtle than one may think. The founding legends of the spiritual traditions—the lives of Jesus, the Buddha, the Baal Shem, Muhammad—portray a struggle of heroic proportions, requiring not only goodwill but extraordinary intelligence, humility, strength of purpose, and courage. And though the inner struggle is neither easy in a way that we might dream of, nor difficult in the ways we might fear, it is first and last a *struggle,* and principally a struggle with oneself, with certain aspects of our own minds, hearts, and bodies. Anyone who has ever undertaken this struggle knows it is far easier to speak about it than to engage in it. The actual difficulty of this struggle cannot, apparently, be put into words or really represented in any way. If there is a hidden wisdom, it lies in the capacity to help men and women understand and confront the actual day-to-day difficulties of this struggle.

And this brings us precisely to the focus of this book. As more and more of us are drawn to the search for a new kind of meaning in our lives, whether on our own or with others, the question naturally arises: Can this search bring a new kind of life to the joys and the demands of living together and working at love?* Can the vision of human nature that underlies the great spiritual philosophies of the world help us sustain the love we all need from each other and which we all need to give to each other? Although there are many books about love and relationships, there are few that try to draw not on the teachings of modern psychology but on the underlying philosophical teachings of the world's spiritual traditions. This book is offered as a modest effort in that direction.

The image of Baucis and Philemon—the old couple—is a symbol not of age, as such, but of mature, sustained love. It is they who open the door to the gods. Jupiter is the lord of the heavens and Mercury is the messenger of divine wisdom. But who is that other god who comes to all of us before they do? Who does not knock gently at our door, but finds us out wherever we are and aims his arrows at us with unerring precision? And why is he smiling in that way?

---

* Although this book speaks mainly about the traditional marriage relationship between a man and woman, it applies equally to any two people who live together and who seek the good for each other.

Chapter Two

THE TWO LOVES

We think we can play with love, but we are mistaken. Love plays with us. It is far more powerful than we are, and if at first we seem to be fitting love into our lives, this is only love's way of smiling at us as we are drawn under its thrall. Lightly, ecstatically, we cross the bridge that love lays down for us. And soon enough we are fighting for our lives.

What can guide us *after* love has set us on fire and we have reentered the world of time and mundane life? The god of love shows us another world. But is it a world we can live in?

We must live together: it is that to which love drives us. The bridge of love has, strangely, led back to where we came from, the world of coming into being and passing away, the world of care and responsibility and action; the world of health and illness, of family, of work and grief and doubt and anxiety and a thousand petty problems and distractions. We have loved and now we must live together; and then, someday, face death.

This book is about the meaning of *sustained love.* What shared purpose is the missing element in our experience of living together? Even with all that has been said and written about human and divine love —from movies and television and the pages of our popular magazines to the inspired poetry of the mystics; from the help offered us by friends, therapists, and counselors, by clergymen and spiritual guides, to sage advice sometimes handed down by parents and grandparents who lived in a time and world so different from ours—what have we still not heard about a shared life in all these writings and teachings and all this common wisdom? What is the deeper purpose of the work of living together within the embrace of love?

It is an urgent question for our culture and our time. Many of the old reasons that kept people together in the past no longer are in force. Reproductive freedom and growing economic independence for women, along with social acceptance of alternative lifestyles, have all displaced the external causes that in the past acted to keep men and women together. Now, with these forces weakened, sometimes to the vanishing point, it must be mainly personal choices that keep us together. And as the enduring power of personal choice turns out to be much weaker than we may have imagined under the first blaze of love, it is no wonder that divorce occupies such a dominant role in our lives. The whole question of being lovers together over time, the shattering instability of what, in pale words, we call "relationships" haunts our lives more and more.

We need to understand what falling in love is really showing us, so that when we have crossed the bridge love lays down for us, we can find the actual meaning of our life together. Hidden in the passion of great love there is a "secret" about why we are on earth at all. This secret can and must unfold in the life we seek to share.

Romantic love carries a taste of freedom from fear and egoism that needs to be understood in the up-and-down process of living together. If we do not understand the larger significance of this freedom, we may never understand what it means to live together in love. This does not mean resigning ourselves to a lesser intensity. On the contrary, the original passion will return again and again. But for many of us, it will do so only if this quieter echo, this hidden teaching that love offers us about ourselves, is heard and attended to.

The social and sexual revolutions of the twentieth century have shown us that relaxing marriage laws and customs, in the end, simply replaced one sort of suffering with another. If we love who and when we want and then break our bond whenever the impulse to do so is strong, we see that it brings no happiness to our lives. Nor, of course, did it bring happiness tensely to maintain the old rules, the old customs. So the meaning of living together in love cannot lie in either direction.

No, we are going to have to perceive romantic love from a rather different perspective. We need to see it, feel it, taste it in both its sensory and super-sensuous meaning, and then follow its echo as it leads us to glimpse the meaning of *sustained love*.

The thesis of this book can be stated quite simply, though it will be no simple matter to draw out its implications. The point is that we human beings are in search of meaning, in search of our selves. Very little of what we already are and already have brings us deeper meaning or happiness. We are born for meaning, not pleasure, unless it is pleasure that is steeped in meaning. And we are born as well for suffering, not the suffering that leads to madness but the suffering that leads to joy: the struggle with ourselves and our illusions. We are born to overcome ourselves, and through that overcoming to find an inner condition of great harmony and being. We are born *for* that—we are not *yet* that. We are searchers; that is the essence of our present humanness.

And in love we have the possibility and the need *to help each other search*. Is this the hidden meaning of the blaze of love, its echo, its teaching? I believe it is. With that echo in mind, we can touch the new sense, practical and full of hope, of sustained love, a purpose that comes not from outworn customs or unrealistic ideals but from our own yearning both for each other and for something within ourselves that is crying to be born.

The First and the Second Love

I am *in love*. The genius of the English language is precise. I am *in* something. And it is carrying me somewhere. I experience the allure and the joy of submission to a force that is outside myself. But, in fact, I am also submitting to aspects within myself, my physical nature, a physical nature which is also a consciousness and a feeling, a sensation that feels and knows. I am in love: the rules of society, the names and borders, no longer limit me. It is a foretaste of what we are meant for. It is nature using our inherent mysticism to join us to the species, to the earth, to all the sensibilities of our terrestrial world.

But what is this other yearning, this other love that can also awaken in me? I may find a certain sweetness in solitude, a certain bittersweet joy in struggling with pain and difficulty. I may be drawn to a specific quality of ideas and symbols that refer to another kind of reality or value system than what society offers me. Or, on the contrary, I may turn away from ideals and symbols and obligations of all kinds. But even when I turn away from them, even when I deny the world of duty and metaphysical aspiration, even then it is from some call within myself that draws me toward struggle and truth and the strange mystery of being myself alone, the seed of *I*, the consciousness of *I*.

The first love, the condition of being in love with another man or woman, we know and can call it by its proper name. But we needn't hurry to give this second love a name. We need only acknowledge—vaguely, but with conviction—that there are two fundamental loves within the human heart, one that draws us to the great forces of the earth, and the other that calls us to search for our selves in the universal world. And the moment we acknowledge these two fundamental impulses, we begin to glimpse the whole challenge of our lives: first, to see these two loves in all their separateness and even opposition; and then, to work for a way to bring them toward each other—to make each love serve the other.

The Names of Love

We divide love and classify it: we discriminate between physical love and spiritual love, between erotic love and personal love, mother love, father love, the love between friends. But the truth is that we remain confused by it. When we are in love, we are in a tornado of forces and all we can do is try to hold on to our chair.

The psychiatrists talk, the therapists talk, the philosophers talk, the novelists talk, the women talk, the men talk, the movies and magazines talk, the singers and musicians talk. Everyone talks about love, but the truth is that our labels are pale efforts to deal with an overwhelming force, as far beyond our control as the wind, the lightning, and the sea.

Could it be that *all* the emotions that whirl us around in our lives are so many fractions of the force of love? Could it be that all feeling is love? That all emotion is love or a derivative of love?

But shouldn't authentic love be kind, compassionate, wise, and tender? Surely such compassionate love is worlds apart from the storm of ecstasy and anguish that we live through when we are in love? Very well, but isn't this ideal of wise and selfless love only that—an ideal, based on a glimpse of an entirely different force that can pass between people?

We talk too much about love—possibly because we live only with half of love, no matter how we break it down and classify it. We live mainly with the half that seeks our own pleasure, or psychological security, or the begetting of children. It is this half of love that brings individuals and nations to their knees, that lifts us up and throws us down. It is this half of love—*because it is only half*, and because it engages only half of the human self—that makes our lives ultimately meaningless. There is another half of love. There is another half of human nature and there is another half of all intimate human relationships.

This other half is the love that helps another search for truth.

Talk about love as much as you wish, read about it, explore it therapeutically, theologically, philosophically. Gossip about it, try to explain it. Spend all the time you wish trying to manage love with words and to ease its contradictions. Only consider: What is really the missing element in our experience of love? If, in our essence, in the heart of our being, we are meant to search for truth; if, as the teachings of wisdom tell us, we are born incomplete, inwardly incomplete, and our possibility is to become complete through an interior struggle —then we cannot avoid asking the question of how men and women can support each other in this struggle.

What is love between people if it does not dwell in the realm of this question?

Intermediate Love

We sometimes suspect that what we usually call love is not really love. We suspect that desire is fundamentally egoistic, that pleasure is for ourselves, not the other. And the pleasure we seek to give to the other—doesn't it really lead back toward our own desires and needs?

But the fact is we experience love as a *mixture* of egoism and care for the other. Perhaps, under certain circumstances, the feeling of care for the other caves in and gives way to some form of selfishness. That does not mean the care for the other is unreal, nor does it mean that it is always and only a disguise, a form of hypocrisy. It may be all that, but not necessarily.

If, when the chips are down, I choose my own welfare over yours, that may only mean that my care for you is weaker than my self-involvement. But to be weak does not mean to be unreal, or to be false, or to be derivative. This is the error of the reductionists—the psychologists and philosophers who try to reduce all human feeling to biology.

Of course, it is equally an error to pretend to ourselves that our care for the other is stronger than our selfishness, our complexified physical desires. But we know about that error. We know now that we are not little tin saints. That error is not the main problem of an era so heavily influenced by psychoanalytic theory.

We need to free ourselves of this "either/or" mentality. Our experience of love is neither saintly nor merely selfish. It is both. But one of these aspects is much stronger than the other.

To repeat: the fact that something is weak does not mean that it is unreal. A weak impulse of care is not an unreal impulse. It is only a weak real impulse.

The fact is that the part or parts of us that are nobler, the "spirit" in us, is almost always weak.

The capacity of selfless love is an aspect of the divine nature in man—and this divine nature is powerless in our lives such as they are. To see this, to accept this, is the very first step toward becoming fully human. To accept this truth is, however, not to accept that this situation must remain. The higher nature *can become* more active, stronger. But the process by which this takes place is inseparable from the effort to see our weaknesses exactly for what they are, without blinders, without cynicism or any other form of self-deception. And this effort is extremely difficult in many ways.

There are fragments of teachings, mystical, Eastern, Western, "esoteric," which tell us that it is easy to accept oneself, to attentively witness one's emotions, one's life. This notion that self-acceptance in its transformative sense is "easy" is, to say the least, misleading. It is difficult, exacting, subtle; we cannot do this work alone. We need help.

Can two people living together as man and

woman, united by the bonds of affection, attraction, physical or emotional type, common interests, or sexual passion—can two such people support this struggle? Can two people help each other to know themselves as two-natured beings who contain the seeds of mysterious possible unity?

I think such help is possible between two people. This help is love.

But it is love of a kind that is never mentioned or described in the literature of love, neither in the psychological gossip of our culture nor in the texts and documents, as we interpret them, of the spiritual teachings of the world.

This kind of love is neither of the earth nor of heaven.

It is neither divine nor "animal."

It is *intermediate love.* It is a love we need more than anything else. Without it all the other kinds of love become either tyrannical or fantastic, taking away our lives in destructive cravings, fears, or pretensions.

The Broken Heart

No sooner do we begin to know other people than we discover their broken heart. Their pain in matters of love. Or their fear, their isolation from love. Or their deadness to love; the sad peace they have accepted in the life of love. The bourgeois compromises or the tense and fragile "happiness" which one holds on to with all the self-deception that the personality can create.

At the same time, the broken heart tells us of a state of the soul that our whole being longs for—and this state of the soul is not necessarily what the personality tells us. When we are in love, or when we love passionately or deeply; when we are happy in love—or even when we only dream of love, imagine love—we are dreaming not only of a fantasy but of a reality. A reality that frees us from ordinary time and space. When we are in love, we touch moments of pure presence—some call it eternity. In love, we taste a condition of freedom, freedom from all that drains and enervates our life, freedom from tensions, anxieties, moods, paranoia, unnecessary emotions of all kinds; freedom from scheming and cunning, from manipulating or exploiting the other.

Of course, it is mixed with other impulses and, of course, sooner or later it almost always crashes, often turning into hatred and sometimes even violence. Or it simply turns tepid or ordinary or bourgeois or "convenient" or whatever—there are a thousand ways that passion fades. And, of course, it is often mixed with absurd, adolescent, or neurotic elements of the personality. It is often "childish." It is often foolish. It levels us and exalts us at the same time—great men and women, calm in their demeanor, wise and important, heavy with serious thought and responsibility: they, too, fall in love and become foolish. Nations fall, wars destroy the lives of millions; history changes because of this.

And so much of the pattern of all human lives reads out as crystallizations around the pain of the end of passion. So much of the life of mankind, so many of the events that define human history are in large part so much scar tissue over the heart.

What Lies Behind
the Sorrow of Passion

The Swiss writer Denis de Rougemont, in his masterful *Love in the Western World*, speaks of the passion of romantic love as a degeneration of the medieval ideal of courtly love, which, in fact, was itself intended to mean spiritual love, the yearning for the growth of the soul.* How to understand this? Perhaps in the inexplicable passion of love there is a vibration from a higher level of human consciousness which is mixed with both the impulses of the body and the socially conditioned emotions, both the animal instincts and the fears and cravings of the ego. Perhaps what we know of sexual love is tinged with an element of the striving toward the One that is the main evolving force of the universe. Perhaps what we experience as sex is, in its most intense forms, already the "burning" of a higher energy.

And perhaps it is true that romantic love is a

---

* Denis de Rougemont, *Love in the Western World*, New York: Pantheon Books, Inc., 1956. See especially Book VI.

degeneration of the mystical ideal of the trouba-
dours—the love of the soul that is symbolized by
woman. Perhaps. But the mystical ideal of the trou-
badours itself may have arisen in part because the
widespread doctrines and practices of Christianity
had by the end of the eleventh century lost much
of their essential feminine element. Both the ideal
of romantic love and the flourishing of the cult of
the Virgin may have arisen partly because the
Church in Europe had become too "muscular" and
judgmental, too absorbed by its capacity to "do,"
and far too little able to conduct the current of
mercy. Outwardly, mercy means forgiveness of sins;
inwardly, it means also the feminine capacity within
each human being to allow in, to receive the healing
forces from above. In this case, the introduction of
the ideal of romantic love may be viewed histori-
cally as an attempt—perhaps lopsided and too easily mixed with alien elements—to return to the
human capacity to receive, allow, open. The cult of
the Virgin was perhaps needed not only for a for-
giving ideology to enter into the mind of Europe,
but also for a sensation to exist in the flesh of
mankind, a sensation that moved inward and not
only outward toward satiety. The experience of ro-

mantic love in its root is the glimpse not only in the mind, but in the body, of the possibility of an interior material transformation of human nature.

Yes, this finer sensation all too easily mixes with fear and ego and imagination. And because of this distortion, it is tempting to regard romantic love only as a human weakness. But beware of taking the distortion for the thing distorted. That breeds cynicism, and cynicism is only another scar over the human heart.

Who Are We, You and I?

Does this tell us anything about what happens when our own individual passions for each other weaken? Or about what to do, how to understand each other when this happens—as it inevitably does, sometimes briefly, sometimes for longer stretches of time, and sometimes permanently?

What carries a relationship through these periods? Many things: trust, friendship, momentum, considerations of security, children, convenience. Other shared passions. The maturity of age and affection. Or strictly negative factors, such as fear of loneliness, fear of guilt, or pathology of many kinds. Or perhaps simply the fact of having made a promise to each other.

And how to know when it is actually time to break the bond, and what does it take actually to take that step? How to know when the change one is seeking is a necessary new movement of life, or when it is only a compelling, but impulsive and ultimately repetitive step backward?

Mere ideas and ideals can only go so far, especially now in an era when the old ideas are losing their authority in our lives—the values and teachings that governed the lives of our ancestors. Once, long ago, these values were mighty forces. Now, they no longer seem to have much power. This seems especially so in matters of love. To honor one's promise or to break it; to hold on to a relationship or to cut oneself free—neither alternative in the long run seems obviously better than the other. Look around us. Who is happy—over the long run—in their relationships, in their loves? The broken heart is almost everywhere.

We need new gods in our lives and in our loving. Or, perhaps, the old gods with new names.

What can we honor in each other beyond the call of passion or habit or momentum or fear? What could be the meaning today of the far ideals that lie at the theoretical basis of the traditions of marriage, such as "one flesh," "spiritual union," or "holy covenant"?

And if marriage or the love between man and woman becomes a "holy covenant," what is holy in it for men and women such as *we* are, in an era such as this in which, for most of us, the gods have retreated?

If it is not only passion, which can fluctuate so markedly; if it is not some "holy" but unrealizable ideal, then what can we cherish in each other—apart from the normally sustained human efforts to care for another's physical and mental well-being?

The answer can only be to regard each other as searchers. This is intermediate love. We cannot really speak of being "one flesh"—our individualistic culture does not, *in fact*, in *practice*, support that vision any longer. We cannot really say that "our souls are one": A soul? The consciousness in ourselves that exists beyond space and time? We cannot even say that we experience that at all.

But we can glimpse another's search. We can be aware of another's struggle for inner freedom, for openness to what is greater within ourselves, and from which we are all cut off by our illusions and our absorption in our fears and desires.

In fact, we will discover—if we look carefully—that when we see each other struggling with ourselves, struggling for inner presence and freedom; when we actually feel this struggle taking place in another person, *we cannot help but love!* Such love is not the love of passion or ego or familial warmth or shared history, or even the mystery of a moment of fused identity. Such love is a hitherto unknown, or, rather, unnamed, capacity that lies within every human being's power. It is love of the human struggle, of that in ourselves which wrestles with ourselves.

It is not love of virtue; it is the love of the struggle for virtue.

It is not love of strength; it is the love of the struggle to confront weakness.

It is not love of the spirit in another, or of the soul in another. It is love for that in another which yearns and struggles for spirit and soul, vaguely understood as these things are.

Such love is not something we "do." It is something that is given to us——from above and from within ourselves.

We are speaking here of the possibility of two worlds, two kinds of love that seem so far apart, coming closer to each other. On the one hand there is the force of the love we all know, and on the other there is the love that is spoken of in the spiritual teachings of the world. Two loves: one exalted and seemingly out of our reach; the other overwhelmingly powerful and in turn ecstatic, anxious, joyous, tormenting. Can we live together in a way that could create an opening for this contact between two worlds, two loves, two kinds of life within ourselves? Is this perhaps the meaning of the tale of Baucis and Philemon——a clue to the puzzle at the end of the story? The two lovers are transformed into everlasting trees: they are no longer individuals in the familiar sense, but universal forces that blend enduringly for eternity. And what they now embody is sustained by another force that is not less but greater than what we usually recognize as conscious selfhood. Perhaps wherever the story originated, it was part of a larger story, of which only hints remain in the tale Ovid tells.

What is clear, however, is that wherever the larger story is told, wherever the perennial wisdom of the world has been transmitted, we hear that we are beings created to bring two worlds together in ourselves, to embody in our conscious life what the New Testament calls *eirēnē*, the bridge that connects the two opposing movements within human nature, "the peace that passeth understanding." Above all, always and everywhere, that which brings the fundamental forces into harmony, that which leads all beings toward unity, is called *love*.

What is the work of love toward each other that can support the search for unity within ourselves? What can we realistically give each other that helps us to be *given to*—by what religion calls God, by what philosophy calls Reality, and by what wisdom calls the Self?

This book is intended to open this question in relation to the actual difficulties we all face in working at love—problems of communication, trust, the pressures of time, and the demands of the bewildering, dramatically changing world in which we all must search for each other and for ourselves.

Chapter Three

COMMUNICATION

When we are falling in love, it is no problem. When we speak, we understand, we hear. When we are silent, we also understand and hear. Communication exists all by itself; there is no problem.

That is the chief miracle of being in love. Suddenly I am heard and it astonishes me. And, equally astonishing, I have the capacity and the will to hear you, to listen to you. It is even a great joy to set aside my own thoughts and surrender to the act of listening to you.

Call it, if you wish, part of the unreality of being in love. But we treat it that way at our peril. When we are in love, we are in a part of ourselves that is separated from the rest of our nature; we are in a part that does not fear, does not worry, a part that feels at home. In love, we approach, we taste, the reality of a great truth, a great idea about the structure of the human being. We taste the idea that in the essence of the human being there lies the act of giving. It is part of the essential structure of a human being to give—to give attention, to give interest, concern for detail and for the well-being of another. These are impulses that are part of our essential nature; we are born with them. They are part of the structure of a human being.

The Western world has come to regard the human being as basically a selfish animal with a complicated brain. And, it is true, most honest evidence of human behavior seems to justify that notion. But wisdom teaches something else: that the evil we do is part of what covers over our authentic inner world, like a thick crust welded to our inner being, like the coat of Nessus that finally destroyed the great Hercules.*

This crust stultifies our lives and prevents our inner being from growing. For, as wisdom also teaches, this inner being of care and attention is like an unborn consciousness. It is there, waiting to be nourished, waiting to be born and grow. But the manner in which we live, the habits of our society, our education, the thoughts and emotions that surround us and shape us, and the way our bodies live without relationship to our inner sensitivity—all suffocates the inner self, and we go through our lives as though it never existed. To break through this crust is difficult—so difficult that the view of the cynics, the view that we are only spoiled animals and little else, seems reasonable and realistic. So difficult, that the notion of the inner divinity of the human being seems like sentimental or religious fantasy.

---

* Slain by Hercules, the dying centaur Nessus tells Hercules' jealous wife Deianira to use the centaur's blood as a charm to prevent Hercules from loving another woman. Deianira anoints a robe with the blood and sends it as a gift to Hercules. The coat causes Hercules intolerable burning pain and fuses to his skin so that it cannot be removed. In the end, the torture of the coat causes Hercules to seek out his own death by fire.

Falling in love is one of the experiences of life that breaks through this crust. There are other experiences also that break through the crust of our conditioned selfhood—great shocks and disappointments, sudden danger, the direct encounter with death, or the deep experience of wonder. In the experience of falling in love, it becomes clear— more so, often, than in these other experiences— that underneath this crust is a consciousness that wishes to and is capable, up to a point, of opening to another human being.

Of course, many other parts of ourselves immediately rush in to obscure this opening. We know that and do not need to recite this fact in great detail again. We know that falling in love is almost always associated with egoistic impulses which are themselves linked, due to our conditioning, to powerful biological forces, social forces, and especially to the nearly universally crippled sexual life in ourselves. We know that falling in love often leads to neurosis in the broadest and most tragic sense of the term.

But if we are very sensitive in our memory, or while it is happening, we may see that falling in love allows something to appear in us for a moment—sometimes brief, sometimes lasting a long time and leading to the threshold of great happiness—that is free, totally free, from the crust of social conditioning that oppresses the being of every one of us. What is this "something"? And what place could it have in the long work of two grownup people living together and working at love?

Listening and the Mirage of Self-expression

The answer to this question, I believe, lies in the discovery, when we are with each other, that the work of listening is the same thing as the work of loving. Forget the names, forget what one usually associates with the words "listening" and "loving." Set aside all memories from school or from childhood about "listening"; set aside all romantic images of "becoming one" and all sexual associations. The need is to experiment with listening as though approaching it from zero. Only keep in mind the possibility of what you may discover—something astonishing: that the power and the ability *and even the will* to communicate, to express oneself, *arises directly out of listening.*

Nothing in modern culture prepares us for this discovery, and so, when it appears, it is even hard to believe or to accept: the capacity of speech arises effortlessly from the intentional renunciation of speech. Or, to put it in another way, the state of listening brings more joy than our usual act of speaking. There are many reasons for this—one being that in listening, in renouncing the impulse to direct the other's attention to myself, I am brought into contact with a quality of attending in myself that my own being thirsts for. It is another kind of process in myself, one that our culture has neglected and has forgotten. This renunciation of so-called "self-expression" can be very quick; some-times it can last only a moment or two, and on the surface it is certainly not even noticed by anyone else. It is an inner act, private.

Anyone who tries this soon discovers how diffi-cult it is—difficult but intensely interesting, full of self-discovery. One discovers that most of the time one is unconsciously listening mainly to one's own thoughts. It takes a certain inner choice to attend for more than a few seconds to the continuity of the other's words and expression. Trying in this way, a man or woman discovers that intentional listening to the other brings about a new kind of listening to oneself. And this kind of self-listening, far from impeding the flow of communication between people, actually allows the beginning of a new quality of exchange.

What Is in Our Words?

Here is the new thing: modern psychology, in both its popular and specialized forms, has not informed us of the different kinds of energy that words can carry. Certainly we must speak to each other and we must help each other be sincere. Certainly we must try to understand what the other is saying—there are many useful methods that can help men and women "interpret" each other's language. But too much emphasis on the content of communication keeps us from discovering the extraordinary spectrum of "electrical" currents that words can carry. And it is not merely a matter of the speaker's "mood" or emotional tone or body language or the inflections in their speech. We're fairly well aware, theoretically, of these factors in communication. What is at issue in communication between people who love goes much farther and deeper down than these factors. *Spoken words can carry a unique quality of attention.* It is a specifically human quality that cannot be imitated. It cannot be duplicated by a machine. It is an essential part of the mystery of speech, that is, the mystery of being human. And it is perceived by the other. Perhaps it is not consciously perceived, but wisdom tells us that there are in every human being faculties that are designed just to receive this kind of perception of the quality of attending that is being directed toward us. We simply do not know the vast spectrum of forces, conscious and nonconscious, human and beyond human, that our organism was built to receive and perceive. Of course, the crust of the conditioned self can be so thick that it prevents these influences from coming into us; or it can prevent us from being aware of these perceptions. The crust of the conditioned self can prevent us from knowing how our own organism is responding to communications from another person.

It goes without saying that the capacity of

words to carry very subtle qualities of human attending has been known for ages by poets. And, certainly, writing is a form of speech. But it is not the same as actual speaking in the presence of another person. One can write with all the sensitivity and inner renunciation in the world, yet speak to another person like an egoistic fool.

Intentional Speech

There is, of course, another kind of renunciation that is essential to authentic communication, and that is the renunciation of silence. But the kind of silence we mean here is more properly called "not speaking" or, simply, repressed speech. The silence of listening is the opposite of repressed speech, and on this point popular psychology has a great deal to offer by showing us again and again how so many seemingly intractable problems of life are actually problems of people fearing to speak to each other, fearing even to try to speak to each other. Obviously, there are massive forces at work here that create this blindness to what is really needed between people. And, obviously, these forces are continuously at work and need to be struggled with again and again. But it is nothing short of a revelation to discover what personal obstacles dissolve when one tries to speak to another person.

Intentional speech almost always costs something to the speaker, that is, it is rooted in some kind of inner sacrifice, inner renunciation. It is *not* the kind of speaking that is more properly called *talking* and that wastes so much of our life. The English language is rich in designations that refer to one or another form of automatic talking— babbling, prating, blathering, gossiping, chattering, and dozens of other words. But *talking*, as opposed to the intentional act of *speaking*, embraces more than what we sometimes refer to by the term "idle talk." Talking can be filled with emotion or it can convey a great deal of knowledge and thought. But it becomes speech only when it is intentional, and it is intentional only when we struggle against the momentum of unconscious self-concealment upon which so much of our lives and our sense of self is based.

At the same time, speaking is not "foolish sincerity." Foolish sincerity is equally an evasion of attentiveness to the other and is often little more than a manifestation of wishful thinking, an abdication of attending to oneself.

All the forms of mere "talking" carry a certain current. They have a certain inner "taste"; they sound a certain kind of note. No conceptual definition alone can define them or test them. It would be quite wrong to judge all such talking in any disparaging way. Most of human life is conducted by means of this talking and many precious or, in any case, uniquely human events take place through this medium. But, undeniably, much that is ugly and horrifying about human life on earth takes place partly because people cannot really discriminate the taste of automatic talking, and falsely value talking only by its apparent content, rather than by the current of attention which it conducts.

Intentional speaking has an unmistakable flavor or quality and, especially with people who are trying to love, it is almost instantly sensed by the other.

Simply put, there is nothing, nothing in the world, that can take the place of one person intentionally listening or speaking to another. The act of conscious attending to another person—when one once discovers the taste of it and its significance—can become the center of gravity of the work of love. It is very difficult. Almost nothing in our world supports it or even knows about it.

It is well and good to read books or hear about love as care for the other. But we become disillusioned with love of all kinds when that care is lacking the element of conscious attending. Of course, there are many levels of this quality of relationship—from our usual brief, rare, momentary flashes of it to the nearly legendary power of love that is manifested in the actions of the great teachers and healers of mankind.

It is something to verify for oneself: love that lacks this element sooner or later brings disillusionment. But it is also to be verified for oneself how even a small amount of this quality, even a trace of it, can bring great life to one's struggle to love another person and to the other's struggle for meaning. When the great religious teachings speak of love, it is love that is based on this quality. When God is mysteriously defined as love,* surely we are being told that the highest forces in the

---

* "He that loveth not knoweth not God; for God is love." (I John 4:8)

universe include this quality of love in its pure and most enduring form, that is to say, love based on intentional renunciation. Isn't it clear that this idea throws much-needed light on the meaning of the story of Christ, a story that resonates with many of the world's great teachings that speak of divinities or higher beings who sacrifice themselves for the sake of humanity?*

Returning to our own lives: it is a great help to try the simple but not-so-easy experiment of dealing with the difficulties of life in terms of the question of communication. In the mundane area of business, for example, one soon finds out that there is practically no problem that cannot be resolved or greatly ameliorated through working with the way people are communicating with each other. And we know very well something of the dimensions of this issue in the field of medicine—the question of doctors and patients communicating

---

* For example, in the Vedic story of Creation, the Cosmic Man (Purusha) is dismembered and the human world comes into being through the process of "re-collection," "re-membering" the parts of the original Man. In Jewish mysticism the God-beyond-God creates the world through the self-sacrifice of "contracting" his own being and through all that flows out (all that is expressed) from Him.

with each other. We know it, painfully, to be true in the relationship between parents and children—to the point of cliché. In fact, when one begins to look at life in this light, one is stunned by the extent, not so much of the difficulties of communication but of the power of communication to heal many of the sorrows of life. It is such a vast issue that one can almost be ashamed that it has not been deeply felt until now. We will come to the conclusion not simply that communication is a means toward love, but, rather, that in a specific sense, communication is love.

Perhaps it seems that everyone knows this nowadays. Isn't everyone speaking about communication? Yes and no. Everyone is speaking about communication, but how many of us are speaking to each other intentionally?

Chapter Four

WHY DO WE QUARREL?

Can we begin by acknowledging that this is an unavoidable aspect of human life together? It is not something that is going to go away; it is not going to be dissolved by psychological insights or philosophical wisdom. Quarreling is here to stay.

Emotional reactions are part of human nature. Take almost any man or woman you know or know of, including the towering historical figures and moral heroes of the past: they, too, quarreled with their spouses. They, too, without doubt, sometimes manifested themselves as petty or spiteful or sullen

or beside themselves with rage or sunk in the histri-
onics of self-pity.

So it is a nearly universal phenomenon. That is
the first thing to acknowledge. But, along with that,
we should recognize that our *attitude* toward these
emotional reactions is not at all supported in the
wisdom teachings of the past. Modern psychology
and psychotherapy takes these reactions very seriously, and many forms of therapy, especially in
their popular expressions, entirely support our general relationship toward such emotional reactions as
irritation, hurt feelings, anger. And what is that
relationship?

It is a sort of attraction, a fascination with
them. Somewhere along the way, we have been per-
suaded to give a great amount of our attention and
concern to these reactions, as though they and they
alone are the main source of our happiness or un-
happiness. These emotional reactions have assumed
enormous importance in our lives. But you will
look in vain for great teachings in any culture or
tradition that give such importance to them.

Does this mean that wisdom tells us to ignore
them? Are we supposed to deny that we feel these
emotions and that we manifest them toward each

other? Certainly not. What is at issue is neither the existence of these reactions nor the pain that they bring. What is at issue is something else—something rather subtle and, actually, unknown to modern psychology.

What to Do About the Ego?

Obviously, if we are searching for inner growth, we must face the question of what to do about the emotions of the ego. And the answer that comes to us from every great inner teaching is that there is something in ourselves that can be free from these emotions. There is a capacity of the mind that can step back from them, a capacity of consciousness to exist independently of the egoistic emotions.

The manner of approaching this capacity and of developing it differs in different traditions, as does the terminology used to characterize emotional reactions. The early Christian ascetics in the deserts of Egypt spoke of these reactions as demons, or "sins": pride, anger, lust, avarice, gluttony, envy, sloth. These "seven deadly sins" were understood psychologically as patterns of emotional re-action which unnecessarily diminish or destroy the capacity of the human psyche to be free. The Buddhists and Hindus often speak of emotional reactions collectively as "the ego"; and the Tibetans, in their powerful image of the "wheel of meaningless life" (the wheel of *samsara*), symbolize the source of inner slavery by the figures of the rooster, the snake, and the pig—the first representing overmastering, self-affirming desire; the second, hatred and anger; the third, immersion in the "mud" of ignorance and untruth. In recent times, the teaching of Gurdjieff has introduced the phrase "negative emotions" to refer to these emotional reactions that play such a destructive role in our lives.

At the core of the great spiritual traditions of the world, however, we are advised not to seek to destroy these emotional reactions, but to allow their existence within the light of our free awareness. There is a long and difficult discipline involved here, an art of intentionally relating to our emotions without, on the one hand, seeking to suppress them, or on the other hand, indulging in their expression. The theory behind this discipline is, in part, that awareness, or pure seeing, can conduct the power eventually to free the human psyche from the pain and disorder of the egoistic emotions.

But whether or not we are engaged in such a discipline and whether or not we envision for ourselves an approach to the ultimate goal that these traditions speak of, the first step along these paths is worth taking very seriously for anyone searching for meaning beyond the level of physical or social satisfaction. This first step involves the cultivation of an attitude toward the emotions that is not common in our society—namely, that they are not "ourselves," that they are processes which need not have the authority in our lives that we usually give them.

The First Power of the Mind

The Stoic philosophers of ancient Rome, both the Phrygian slave Epictetus and the emperor Marcus Aurelius, spoke of this attitude of the mind toward our emotional life. What defines us as human beings, they said, is the capacity of our mind to deal consciously and intentionally with the impressions and experiences that life brings us. These teachings of the Stoics have often been misunderstood as advocating a sort of indifference or coldness. But a more careful study of these teachings and of others connected to them shows that what is being spoken of is a fundamental power of the mind to separate itself from the confusion and disorder of the egoistic reactions that drive our lives around and around and which are so destructive in our relationships with each other. In fact, the Stoic teaching, if looked at carefully, tells us that it is actually through separating from these emotional reactions that we begin to approach the real power of the mind, not only to see clearly but to love truly, to care truly, and even, in a sense, to hate truly—that is, to "hate" what is truly evil and not merely what goes against our subjective desires or which provokes our subjective fears.

Starting with Thought

What does this mean in practical terms? As a place to begin, it means the cultivation of a certain orientation of thought during the periods when our emotions are less agitated. How do we *understand* these common and troubling occurrences between men and women who are trying to love each other?

We hardly ever think this way about the phenomenon of quarreling. We hardly ever consider the importance in our everyday lives of the ideas we hold about the nature of our mind. We have been told by the prevailing modern psychology that our happiness and well-being depends mainly on our emotions. Or, perhaps, we have heard about spiritual doctrines that tell us we are inwardly divine and capable of pure love. But neither of these views is of help when negative emotions are actually activated. I have seen many sulking Buddhists, resentful yogis, and pouting Christian mystics.

Almost everyone quarrels and almost everyone is disturbed by these quarrels. But two people who are living together and trying to love can help each other by a shared understanding of the nature of the emotions—both their overwhelming power when they are active and their overall *secondary reality* in the developing human being, in the man or woman who is searching for an inner life.

The gods then, as was but right, put in our hands the one blessing that is best of all and master of all, that and nothing else, the power to deal rightly with our impressions, but everything else they did not put in our hands. Was it that they would not? For my part I think that if they could have entrusted us with those other powers as well they would have done so, but they were quite unable. . . .

But what says Zeus? Epictetus, if it were possible I would have made your body and your possessions (those trifles that you prize) free and untrammeled. But as things are—never forget this—this body is not yours, it is but a clever mixture of clay. But since I could not make it free, I gave you a portion in our divinity, this faculty of impulse to act and not to act, of will to get and will to avoid, in a word the faculty which can turn impressions to right use. If you pay heed to this, and put your affairs in its keeping, you will never suffer let nor hindrance, you will not groan, you will blame no man, you will flatter none. What then? Does all this seem but little to you?*

The point is that wisdom tells us of another capacity within ourselves, the possibility of a life that is not at the beck and call of our subjective emotions. It is a life of mind, and of intense, but nonagitated, feeling. It is our possibility—and, wisdom tells us, a human being cannot be fulfilled without the cultivation of this possibility. Anything else that passes for happiness is at best hedged in by tension or by self-deceptions that are inevitably exploded. This pseudohappiness is what the ancient teachings sometimes call "pleasure." "Pleasure," we are told, can bring happiness only to the extent that it is free from fears and illusions about who and what we are and what our future will be and what the well-being of others consists of.

A man or woman, a human being, is built,

* *The Stoic and Epicurean Philosophers: The Complete Extant Writings of Epicurus, Epictetus, Lucretius, Marcus Aurelius.* Edited, and with an Introduction by Whitney J. Oates, New York: Random House, 1940. First Modern Library Giant Edition, 1957, p. 224.

structured, for the happiness that comes from the cultivation of a deeper power of mind and feeling than is offered to us by the automatic processes of emotional reaction.

At the same time, these emotional reactions are overwhelmingly powerful when they are taking place.

It is important to have more accurate thought about the nature and function of these emotions. Such thought can be developed and can be entertained in our minds *in between the occasions of emotional agitation.* The point is, the question is—odd though it may sound: *How to think about quarreling in between the quarrels?* And how to support—silently perhaps, and with actions and with one's general state—the struggle of the other person to discover and maintain an attitude toward the emotions that corresponds more precisely to their real nature and place in the life of men and women searching for themselves?

We Are Human Beings

Silently—or, perhaps, sometimes in words, but not too many words—you and I understand that, before everything else, we are human beings in search of our Self. We are human beings: this cosmically unique being whose essence contains the whole of nature and nature's God. We are built to contain very fine, very subtle, and creative elements, the current that sustains worlds; we are also built to contain all the powers and urgings of the animal and of the matter of earth. Wisdom tells us we are both—god and animal, heaven and earth—at one and the same time, and through the existence together of these levels something of God is meant to enter into the world of humanity and the world of our planet. That is what we are, cosmically, as human beings. And we are two in another sense—a related sense, but not exactly corresponding to this cosmic structure. We have in ourselves the yearning to actualize this authentic destiny, and we have in ourselves overwhelming and massive ignorance of this yearning and what it strives for. We have in ourselves a spark of divine hunger, along with an inferno of fear and tension that calls itself desire, but which is often actually normal physical and social desire mixed with unconscious terror—what the Buddhists call "craving"; what the Christians once called "passion." We are both an expansive thrust upward and a dark contraction downward; we wish and we do not wish for the Self. And much of our emotional life falls on the side of ignorant opposition to the process of self-knowledge.

We are human beings. Before we are man or woman, we are human. Before we are rich or poor, father or mother, we are human. Before we are frightened or foolish or forgetful or fine or coarse or anything at all, we are human. We are human with a human possibility and a human destiny: we can become a new being before we die. We wish for that, you and I; and we do not wish for it. We are human.

Thoughts such as these, articulated with much more precision and completeness, and with much more beauty and power, can be found in the writings of the great philosophers, poets, and spiritual teachers of the past and present; these truths can be seen in the images of art and can be sensed directly in certain kinds of music that have been given to the world. But such thoughts, and the ideas they point to, are not only to be entertained in moments of quiet reflection, as a means of carrying ourselves away from the realities of everyday life. Such thoughts can be brought into awareness even when there is no impulse to do so; when the problems of living together are tearing at us, when we are troubled with ourselves and each other—*in between the moments of great agitation.*

Such thoughts can be more than solace and can do more than lead us into a more "spiritual" mood. They can inform our mind and body and emotions that there is, as it were, "someone else" in our house, "someone" important. That is, there is another aim possible in my life and in your life. The work of love in this case consists in remembering that you have both a wish and a resistance. Our work consists in remembering this about each other —not only that we are the father or mother of our children and that we have a shared past and have had wonderful moments together, and so on. That is all important, of course. But what we are speaking about here is another kind of remembrance, a remembrance that you will not find described in the popular psychology of our time, a metaphysical remembrance of who we are and what we seek to be and what lawfully stands in our way.

Can intentionally harboring such thoughts actually help the life of living together? Is anyone trying it?

Chapter Five

TRUST

It is possible to view the crisis of the modern world as a crisis of trust. If we ask in what does our culture as a whole place its trust, we will not find an ennobling answer. For many of us, this crisis of trust is reflected in what we may term, using a phrase coined by the sociologist Anthony Giddens, "ontological insecurity." Down deep, we do not trust the world or life or what is called reality. And more and more, on the deeper emotional levels, we do not trust other people, not even those who are close to us. On the deep emotional level, many do not even trust their parents. Perhaps something of this has always been so. Wisdom tells us that in the end there is nothing to trust but God —not God as the external projection of our anxieties and dreams, but the actual reality above and within ourselves. Wisdom has always taught that everything else is ephemeral, not to be trusted beyond a certain point. This is the essential message of Judaic monotheism: trust only in the ultimate, in God. Easy to say, but what does it really mean in practice? The fact is, most of us do not deeply, safely trust either in something above ourselves or in each other. Much of what passes for trust is untested and brittle.

But when we fall in love, there is often, if only briefly, a miraculous sense of coming home. Home is where we can let down our guard. Here, finally, we are safe.

Or are we? What is this anxiety that for so many of us follows along with love? What is it we crave when we anxiously seek, again and again, to be reassured that we are first in the heart of the other? Is there something here that needs to be understood—not as a neurotic symptom, but in the light of what the teachings of wisdom tell us about the human condition?

Wisdom teaches us that we cannot expect of an ordinary man or woman what is only a property of an inwardly developed human being. We err in expecting the other to be steadfast or whole in a way that we know, in our sincere moments, we ourselves can never be. We seem to expect of the other what we ourselves could not give. This is why even the very beginnings of honest self-knowledge bring, automatically, a certain degree of tolerance for others. In the moments when we honestly see how we ourselves are, we have the possibility of not demanding from another that which the other cannot give.*

Looking at ourselves honestly, we can observe that human steadfastness—trustworthiness— comes only very rarely from an inner freedom of will and sustained self-mastery. It is much truer to

---

* *All real self-knowledge brings love and compassion with it.* The reason for this is that, as it is said in the teachings of wisdom, the human self is intrinsically relational, intrinsically caring and open to life. This is Buddhism, this is Hinduism, but it is also the Christianity of a Meister Eckhardt and the Judaism of the Kabbalah and the Hasidic *rebbes.* This view of human nature contradicts the accepted views of our day, from Freudian psychoanalysis to the latest theories of evolutionary psychology, which regard human nature as intrinsically egoistic.

say that it comes from obedience to rules which have been imposed on us from the outside or injected into us as "morality" in childhood. The moral systems we are brought up with and which form the basis of our social order can therefore actually be read as so many "scripts" for more developed human beings—or, alternatively, as the traces of experiences left for us by more inwardly developed men and women. As such, this morality rightly commands our respect, but it would be foolish to assume that psychologically, inwardly, we ourselves correspond to these moral systems. We may ask that another person keep promises to the same extent that we ourselves keep promises. But we are dreaming dangerous dreams if we imagine that the other person is some kind of saint.

Our lives, individual and collective, show us that we have overestimated ourselves with respect to our inner capacity for moral behavior. It is not only that we see every nation and people, including America, acting in ways that are unendurably immoral; we see it in our own lives as well. Therefore, one of the central aspects of the search for ourselves is to become honestly aware of the real nature of our morality and to become free of the illusions about ourselves that accompany both moral fervor on the one hand and the cynical denial of the claims of morality on the other.

But all this does not yet get to the heart of what we really are craving when we nervously long to be able to have more trust in the man or woman we love. We have not yet answered the question: What is the anxiety that so often accompanies the state of being in love and which also often remains as a problem in the work of living together? What is the anxiety that is at the root of the passions of jealousy and suspicion?

What Do We Really
Want from Each Other?

Bluntly stated, what we often demand of others is that they be devoured by their feelings for us. We feel safe only when the other is obsessed by us. When the obvious signs of obsession are absent, we begin to worry.

We see this situation not only in relationships between men and women, but almost everywhere in our lives. We take anxiety and obsession as a sign of caring; our world often demands a kind of fanaticism as proof of our commitment. How often are we compelled in this respect to bluff about our feelings—not only in relationships, but at our jobs and in many of the situations of our communal life. Society encourages us to be, or at least to act, addicted. And without any other authentic vision of the meaning of care in front of us, this acting often *makes* us addicted. Our world favors a kind of insanity.

We have ambiguous feelings about the capacity for another man or woman to be calm. On the one hand, we are troubled when someone we love or who works with us is not torn up by his or her feelings about us or about what we care for. On the other hand, we are touched by the power of great men and women to radiate an inner collectedness in situations that would bring most people to panic or excesses of zeal. And, certainly, in any emergency, we want our leaders to keep their heads.

Love and Agitation

The fact is that throughout history, the great models of the power to love are men and women who are both deeply committed to others and detached at the same time. The accounts of Christ and the Old Testament prophets show us passion directly solely against forces that stand in the way of the truth—whether it is Jesus angrily driving the money changers out of the temple or Isaiah denouncing King Ahaz's alliances with the Assyrians. And there can be no doubt of the passionate devotion of Gautama Buddha, and those who continued the transmission of his teaching, in giving all their heart and energy to helping others toward inner freedom. The life of Muhammad and the lives of the teachers of Sufi wisdom are filled with fervor and total commitment to the good of humanity. Yet nowhere do we see even the slightest instance of such individuals losing their heads, acting impetuously, or panicking under conditions of impending defeat and crisis. How is it, for example, that Socrates speaks so calmly to his beloved pupils as he is about to swallow the hemlock that will kill him? Why are their personal anxieties and emotions so summarily brushed aside? The poet and Sufi master Rumi loves, as we shall see, with as much anguish and longing as any star-crossed lover in history or myth; but never is his love personal, never for his own subjective well-being alone—his love is always a mysterious fusion of passionate self-forgetting and deeply sober self-remembering. In the same Sufi tradition, the teacher al-Junayd in the tenth century even upbraids the famous al-Hallaj, who was martyred for his extreme expressions of mystical truth, for losing his sobriety. Yet, like all the great Sufi teachers, Junayd was also a teacher of spiritual love.

If we look at such individuals and the accounts written about them, we will see that the quality of their love was never addictive or fanatical; their fervor was of a kind that was often incomprehensible to those around them—that is, utterly nonegoistic and impersonal. In the midst of their fervor, a certain mysterious stability and calm prevailed.

Wisdom tells us that deep in ourselves there is a consciousness that can love impartially and that calls us to serve purposes beyond our biological and socially conditioned needs and desires. When we sense in another person that his or her main motivation is to come into contact with this deeper consciousness and to obey it, *we cannot help but trust that person*. On any level, when we see a man or woman who sincerely seeks to serve something nonegoistic, something nonfanatical, something that we sense is for the common good, we cannot help but trust such a person. We spontaneously trust people who are not out for themselves.

What Can We Trust in Each Other?

What is the practical meaning of this more authentic meaning of trust? It is a question of what we address ourselves to in each other. When we call to someone, to whom are we calling? To what in them? What in any of us can be steady, stable, unchanging? There is an answer to this question, and the answer is not cynical. Nor is it the answer given by some interpreters of mystical religion. Nor is it the answer given by various schools of modern psychology.

The answer, I believe, is that we can trust the lawful nature of the human search for the self. A man and a woman can greatly help each other feel that this search is more to be trusted than anything else in life and that without this search—and the moments of reality it brings—all the other goods of life will sooner or later turn bitter or empty.

It is precisely because the apparent goods of life showed themselves as untrustworthy that we first undertook to look for something deeper than what is offered by the world around us. It is the teaching of wisdom, and it is what we discover for ourselves, that the world we know cannot offer us real love, safety, well-being, bonds of true loyalty, peace. If it were otherwise, why would we search? Yet everything in our surroundings conspires to persuade us that there, outside of our inner self, lies the possibility of these goods of life. As the wise teachers of old told us, the world is like a market-place with everyone hawking their wares: Ecstasy! Salvation! Reputation! Freedom from fear! Honor and respect! The gratitude of children! The legacy of accomplishment!

We can trust the inner struggle in each other— that is to say, we can trust the laws and forces that come into play in human life when there is an inner struggle for the truth about ourselves. When an individual falls into fear or anger or self-pity, these emotions—like small children—strive to evoke emotions in the other of a similar nature. The state of emotional "capture" strives to create "capture" in the other. But if a man or woman trusts that, under the surface, the other yearns to rediscover his or her search, then something new can take place between two people. If, in the midst of emotional difficulty, one person remembers the inner search, the other may also remember—not immediately, perhaps; and it probably will not have the power to harmonize the turbulence. But it can be trusted that the process of remembering one's inner search, faint and intermittent though that remembering may be, will have an effect. No one ever regrets undertaking this kind of struggle right in the midst of emotional difficulty. No one ever regrets sacrificing attachment to unpleasant emotional reactions.

And if an individual senses that his or her search is trusted by the other, this alone can bring into a relationship a current of love of a quality that can be brought in no other way. If an individual is regarded as *one who is seeking*, it brings an element of mutual respect that is unlike anything else that ordinary life can bring.

What Do We
Respect in Each Other?

Certainly people need to be appreciated and respected for what they are in all the aspects of human nature. But to respect and trust each other as companions on the way, companions in the search, offers to our modern life a wholly different meaning of trust and respect. Without this kind of trust and respect, the other kinds do not bring happiness because they are not based on the complete truth. We need to be respected as men and women, as mothers or fathers, and for what we have learned and practiced in our life activities, in our jobs or careers; we need to be respected as human beings without complicated philosophical or theological justification. We are human beings; we must respect each other: whether we are aware of it or not, the voice of conscience is always telling us that. And trust is at the core of respect—not blind trust that blinks at weaknesses, but the trust in something higher that can act through human beings over and above personal needs and desires—trust in the human being as, in Nietzsche's words, "the animal that can make promises."

But Nietzsche might also have said: "A human being is the animal that can break promises." Because we see that we cannot trust each other past a certain point. That is fact. So throughout our lives our sense of each other will continually be dual: we respect each other, while at the same time continually monitoring the level of trust we can place in each other as we actually are. I respect your divinity; I distrust your demons. Just as, if I am struggling for my inner truth, I respect my own divinity while trying to be sincere with myself about my own demons.

The Transformation of Trust

Can there be no resolution of this contradiction? Must we be tossed between these two attitudes toward each other and toward ourselves? The answer is that it is possible to find a unitary single-minded attitude toward each other and toward ourselves. There can exist an impulse in every human being that spans both sides of our human nature without making us pretend we are either better or worse than we are. *We are searchers.* A searcher is aware that he or she is a two-natured being. And that the other is the same. Each one of us both is and is not. Each one of us can become for the other a haven from the power of the world to suggest to us that we are more or less than we actually are. We can protect each other from the power of everyday life to encourage attachment. As the teachers of wisdom tell us and show us by their lives: agitation is never the same as care; tension is never strength; fanaticism is never commitment; egoism is never greatness; fearfulness never brings safety; self-pity never attracts real compassion. The life of the world may persuade us to honor such self-centered emotions and treat them as representatives of our inner self. But two people trying to love each other can bring to each other the comfort and tranquillity that comes from being seen and loved as *both* weak and strong at the same time. Two people can help each other *remember*—not by words or even, necessarily, by actions, but by their own remembering at the moments when the other is in a difficulty. Every man and woman needs tenderness, laughter, acceptance, assurance, and loving intimacy. But every man or woman in search of truth needs most of all to remember who we are and what we are searching for—and why. When two people try to help each other in this way, the meaning of trust is transformed.

Chapter Six

TIME

We all know what happens to time when we fall in love. When we are with each other, it can seem that we have no past or future, that there is no such thing as time and its limitations. And when we part, even after hours or days of great intensity, it is as though we have hardly been together at all: time is all too real, all too precious, and we have too little of it. And often, when we are together and feel the exquisite value of the time we have, we may try to hold it still, to reach culminations that we hope will protect us from the world of time that waits for us tomorrow or the day after in our ordinary life. In love, we know, we *know*, that time is not what we thought it was. We know we have lived our everyday life under the sway of a master who pretends to an authority which is not what it seems. In a way we do not understand, we know the power of time depends to some extent on something in our own minds. But what that something may be we do not know and we do not know the way to reach it intentionally. The temporality of love remains pure gift, pure grace.

Two Kinds of Time

But when a man and a woman are living together, they are no longer only looking at each other; they are looking out at the world. Whether they want to or not, lovers who live together are compelled by the world to look away from each other. This necessary turning to the outer world, to the demands of everyday life, takes a man or woman into the process of the way the world experiences time. A man and woman will return again and again to each other and, again and again, they may experience the temporality of love. But their lives now will be under two fundamental qualities of time, two temporalities: the temporality of love and the temporality of obligation. It is obligation, demand, duties, necessities that draw us away from the temporality of love.

Wisdom teaches that what lovers experience as freedom from the tension-ridden temporality of the world is, to some extent, a transformed inner state, a taste of mankind's psychological birthright. In the intensity of being in love—to some extent, and not always and not with everyone—we experience both the body's pure given-ness to the purposes of nature *and* the psyche's pure movement of obedience to the touch of a reality beyond the ego.

We need to look at this situation, setting aside for now the fact that the egoistic personality, shaped by the distortions of modern education, immediately exploits this experience through fear and makes being in love into something nervous or dreamy or obsessive. Looking at the temporality of love, it becomes clear that it involves a transformed relationship between the mind and the body.

The Reality and
the Unreality of Time

Many philosophers have told us that time, which seems so real, is actually a projection of our minds. This is an intriguing idea, but very few of us actually can say we have verified it. Vaguely, indistinctly, we know that the experience of time depends on something in us, but it is only an intriguing concept. It does not really help us in our lives. When the demands of life with all their anxieties and fears, all their exaggerated promises, invade us, the pressures of time seem all too real. And these pressures seem often to keep us from each other. We do not have enough time for each other. More and more, this problem is seen as a central problem of love in our era. So let the philosophers and the masters of wisdom say what they will; time seems very, very real.

But perhaps we have not seen the whole of what the great teachings are telling us about the subjectivity of time. Because, in fact, the experience of passionate love can show us something about time that perhaps has not been seen in its real significance. In the passion of love, there can be a completely new relationship between the mind and the body. It is not just that our bodies are exquisitely alive, filled with the power of nature. It is often thought of in this way and described in this way by poets and novelists. But, in fact, what is often taking place is actually a new, more conscious relationship between the body and the mind. We are so accustomed to the qualities of the mind in its absent or tormented relationship to the body that when a natural, unforced relationship appears between the mind and the body, we call it an experience of the body alone. But the passion of love is more accurately characterized as an experience of a "harmonic resonance" between the mind and the body. And note—when we say "mind," we are not saying only the intellectual capacity. Because obviously, there is, and this above all, a new experience of the feeling function in us. Mind, body, and feeling approach each other—for a moment, for a brief moment—in a way they rarely do otherwise.

And time is transformed. We can say, then, subject to our own personal verification, that the experience of time depends not exactly on the mind but on the relationship between the mind and the body. There may be much more to it than this, obviously. And much more knowledge, a vast immensity of knowledge about this element of time, is offered in the detailed teachings of the great wisdom traditions. But for us, perhaps, this insight is enough to allow us to begin a practical study of how two people can help each other in facing together the problems of love that are associated with time and its pressures.

The first step in such a study is obviously to come to grips with one's own relationship to time. One needs one's own personal examination of how anxiety of all kinds is rooted in anxiety about time, how the factor of time enters into every tension, every fear, every gnawing desire of our lives. It is there, in every cell of our emotional life. We need to look for it and see it for ourselves, impartially. Along with this study, it is equally essential to take account of one's own relationship to the body, that is, to the current of organic life that is always present in the tissues of our body but which we are usually aware of only in rare moments of passion or physical pain. There is in the body a flowing deep river of tangible sensitivity about which our culture has told us nothing. A human being's intentional relationship to this current determines a great deal about both the normality of our day-to-day experience and the real possibilities of the inner search. It is necessary to see, personally, how even a faint and fleeting intentional opening to this current of organic sensitivity frees us from so much of the tyranny of time. One also sees, much more deeply, how often we lose this relationship to the body, and how much of deeper life, deeper feeling, more balanced intelligence we lose when we are under the sway of the temporality of the world—the temporality of a world without a life-inside-the-body.

Love and Presence

Seen from this point of view, it becomes possible, perhaps, to face the modern problem of time in a new way. We can ask ourselves, and help each other ask: Do we ever really feel overwhelmed by the pressure of time, when even to a small degree the mind is consciously inside the body? This is a serious matter for exploration: Is it true that we can never be really agitated when we consciously inhabit our bodies?

To the extent that our culture moves us more and more to be able to satisfy the material demands of life with little or no need for an intentional relationship to the body, isn't it inevitable that we are afflicted with the disease of busyness and haste? Almost every new technical application of the modern world is considered a mark of "progress" because it relieves people of the need to attend to the body while pursuing the tasks of life. The computer is only the latest and most influential of these new technologies. The problem of time in the modern world is therefore, to a great extent, the problem of living in the head.

There is much more to this. When we live so much in the head, the body does not disappear; it simply goes its own way, doing what it likes to do, like an uncontrolled domestic animal. And the feelings, without intentional relationship to the rest of the self, run wild like abandoned little children.

In any case, more and more the problem of time bedevils people trying to live together in love. With or without the demands of raising children, most people have too little time for and with each other.

It is only common sense, of course, to try to correct this situation in obvious ways—vacations, weekends, evenings together. We do not need the wise teachings of the world to tell us that.

But in the light of all that we have said, there are subtler ways that we perhaps can help each other. What happens to the experience of time between two people when one of them is less under the sway of agitation? When you are calm—not like a stone, of course, nor like a pseudo-saint— what becomes of my busyness and haste?

Of course, there is, as we have already discussed, a strange and sometimes amusing aspect of human nature: one can actually resent it when another person refuses to be agitated by one's own anxieties. It is as though the other person doesn't care enough or understand the situation. But authentic quiet in a man or woman results not in removal but in openness and compassion toward the other. Compassion does not mean one is mortally infected by the other's fear or hurt.

The point is that whatever may happen in the short run, in the long run one person's state can remind the other of what he or she is searching for. A person's state is not the same thing as mood or emotional reaction. It has to do mainly with the degree to which a person is *there*, present in the moment. To be present in the moment is to be in an intentionally open relationship to the body. The mind alone is never really *here*; never really *now*. It is only mind and body together that, in any significant sense, can exist in the present moment and be free from the tyranny of time.

And that, surely, is what we are searching for when we search for a life that transcends the hypnosis of the world: freedom from the tyranny of time. The traditions use a great word, "eternity," when speaking about this goal. But whatever this word may mean in its depths, practically speaking we approach the sense of this word in the temporality of love when a sense of the eternal is experienced as pure gift. But here, as elsewhere, what is experienced as gift when we fall in love is to be taken as an invitation to work intentionally toward a whole life that is open to this gift in even far greater quality and degree.

Chapter Seven

MONEY, WORK,
SEX, POWER,
BEAUTY ... LIFE ITSELF

If one were to attempt the impossible task of summing up in a few words the message of all the wisdom teachings of the world, it might be: *the meaning of life is not to be found in life itself but beyond life.* The idea is that life, ordinary human life as we know it, proceeds at the mercy of influences which have nothing to do with the inner development of individual human beings and which, looked at in a certain way, may even be opposed to our development. At the same time, there exist other forces and influences in the world that favor and support our inner growth. These favoring influences, we are told, come to us through men and women who embody an exceptional purity of intelligence and love and an exceptional capacity to help others search for their own Self. Out of this second kind of influence, great spiritual traditions and schools of wisdom have arisen throughout history, and these traditions and schools have in turn attempted to transmit to mankind the knowledge of what is called the *Way*.

These two kinds of influences exist side by side in the life of mankind. Although they exist side by side, however, they are nevertheless quite different and distinct and are *felt* as such by many people. Usually, we cannot give a clear account to ourselves of this difference, but we feel it and we often sense this same feeling or attraction in another man or woman. An individual is drawn to certain kinds of ideas, or music, or art, or is concerned with certain kinds of questions that are not especially honored in the general turnover of life. And when we meet another man or woman who is similarly drawn, it is often the most essential aspect of the birth of love between two people, even more essential than sex or other kinds of motivating forces.

A Shared Life and a Shared Search

This aspect of falling in love is not simply a question of "common interests"; it is a matter of a certain, very specific *kind* of interest, a specific quality of hope in the search, and also, very often, a specific quality of disappointment with all that ordinary life has to offer, a disappointment with what money can buy, with the goals of fame, power, or prestige, with the advertised satisfactions of cosmetic beauty and physical attraction, a disappointment, even, with conventional religious, moral, aesthetic, and scientific values. The modern world has tended to regard this sort of interest with skepticism—and perhaps rightly so, in many cases. It is certainly true that people can deceive themselves about their so-called higher motivations. And it is certainly true that even people who have this special kind of interest strongly developed in them also have within themselves just as much of the other sort of motivations as anyone else. We may be drawn to each other through a shared feeling of search, yet at the same time we are as driven as the rest of mankind by our sexual needs and by the impulses of vanity or ambition or fear. Once again, falling in love even in its most exquisite forms represents no more than a taste and a promise of a more profound quality of conscious life. If lovers themselves tend to overestimate the purity and durability of this taste, then the modern "realistic" view of love, which is aware of all that is mixed in with romantic love, tends to underestimate the contact with higher human possibilities that being in love gives to almost everyone at least once in his or her lifetime.

This said, when a man or woman who is searching, often beneath the level of awareness, for something apart from the values and forms of life as we know it meets another man or woman in whom the same search exists, the experience of falling in love has an exceptional dimension that goes beyond the sexual, social, or psychological aspects of human relationships. The challenge is to maintain this quality of connection in the work of living together.

It is not only a matter of two people maintaining the sense of search that was such an important element in drawing them together. It is much more than that. The point is that when two people are drawn to each other in this way, they have the possibility—and perhaps the duty—not only to maintain this quality of relationship but to help each other deepen the search and carry it forward in each other's individual life.

Beyond "Life Itself"

We are not speaking of people trying to be each other's guru. But when a man and woman begin to live together, all the forces of life, all the influences of human life on earth—from which one was to some slight extent freed in the passion of falling in love—enter into one's life with renewed power. And they are experienced as problems, as difficulties, and, sometimes, as obstacles to love. Through these influences, lovers often begin to drift apart from each other or to hold on to each other with neurotic obsession. These influences of "life itself" are invariably reflected by a movement toward fragmentation and disunity, a movement toward isolation or conflict. To appreciate this fact, it is only necessary to remember what the world has suffered through the cravings for wealth, for security at the expense of others, for political or religious power, for unrestricted sex, for fame and adulation.

And yet every human has social and psychological needs. Every human being is both a social self and an embryonic soul. The challenge of life is to support the former while nourishing the latter. It is not easy. On the contrary, it is all too easy to imagine one is nourishing the soul while actually indulging the power of the social self, that is, making the normal social self into the cosmic anomaly that the wisdom tradition calls "the ego."

How to help each other remember that there exists something beyond "life itself"? The fact is that modern psychology, in both its professional and popular forms, is almost entirely lacking in this idea.

This is not to forget that modern psychology was born from the healing recognition and acknowledgment that human beings have legitimate needs for sex, for appreciation, for success, for self-respect, for material security, for a sense of acceptance and place in the social order. A dogmatic and hypocritical religious establishment was eventually forced to submit to these truths, which were with some difficulty brought into the life of our culture by the founders of modern psychiatry and psychology. But the retreat of religion went so far as to turn over to psychology the whole idea of the nature of the self, and much of our religion lost all sense of its roots in the wisdom tradition that speaks of that in us and in the universe that is higher than "life itself." Psychology's healing insights and methods were never intended and never were able to address the "verticality" of the human psyche. And everything it now offers people, especially in its popular forms—and what we could call the generally accepted views of our society—tends to push people into giving more weight than is necessary to the social/biological needs and desires —to good looks, health, sexual pleasure, success, family responsibilities, career.

As for popular morality in its many forms, although its dicta refer to other obvious normal aspects and obligations of humanity, it places more weight than is necessary on the goals of ethnic or gender solidarity, for example, or patriotism, political opinions, "causes" of all kinds, many of which mask impulses of fear and self-interest. Life presents these psychological and moral ideals in forms and ways that lure individuals into the state that we have already spoken of as "attachment." Through attachment, nothing beneficial for mankind ever enters the world or an individual human life. To be disappointed in "life" means, first and foremost, to be disappointed in the manner in which society's ideals and goals turn people, through attachment, toward conflict, isolation, and sentimentality. A great many people, even from early childhood, sense the hypocrisy and shallowness of the goals of society. Without knowing how to explain it to themselves, they sense that "life itself" is based on lies and is going nowhere, that it is what Plato called "the world of appearances" or what the Buddhists call "the wheel of birth and death."

Again, how can two people help each other remember what is primary and what is secondary in their lives, that is, in all human life in its essential structure? The power of "life itself" is especially strong for people living together and trying to love each other. The legitimate and normal needs together with their distortions due to our unawakened state operate on each other mutually: the need for approval, which can become the obsession for being right; the need for compassion and tenderness, which can become the cravings of self-pity; the need for sexual love, which in the myriad obsessional forms that are thrust upon us all by our modern upbringing can become a veritable theater of anxiety and tension with its jealousy, fear, guilt.

At the same time, although the power of "life itself" is especially concentrated with two people living together, it is also true that two people living together can be to each other a greater source of help than almost any other source. Two people together can help each other maintain their personal struggle to stay open to influences in life that favor inner growth. These favoring influences may be a teaching that they follow, or it may be a special individual whom they respect as a source of guidance and special knowledge, or it may be simply a shared "magnetic" resonance with certain kinds of ideas or practices, such as meditation, or art, or the interest in relatively unspoiled ancient traditions at the heart of other cultures.

Love and the Hypnosis of Life

The point is that a relationship is like a small world all by itself. In the world at large the seductive, hypnotic influences of life are completely separate from the influences that favor inner freedom. But in a relationship between two people sharing the search, each one can act on the other in a way that brings one in front of a much broader range of human possibility. I may, for example, be anxious about what you think of me, but if you are, in that moment, inwardly quiet, if—for that moment— you do not allow my anxiety automatically to frighten you, too—which automatic reaction is what constantly happens in "life," and which reaction and all that follows in its train brings so much agitation and suffering to mankind—if, to repeat, through your own search you in that moment are calmer inside, then I am immediately helped to discover a certain "space" around my own fear, and I may find that I am able not to feed my fear with all my automatic attention. In a word, two people can help each other become free of the reactions of life that they inevitably evoke in each other. A relationship is like a little world and can be like a tiny fragment of a "spiritual community" within that world.

If I crave egoistic recognition from the world, I also will crave it from you. If I crave the world's pity, I will also crave it from you. If I crave the appearance of success, I will also crave it from you. But you need not be completely like the world to me. You need not persuade me that unless I believe myself to be preposterously great, or beautiful, or powerful, then I am worthless—or something to that effect. In your words and actions, and especially in your state of inner search, you can help me dissolve these fears and tensions which are based on the ingrown hypnotic education that the world and society give me from earliest childhood, and which it continues to give me through all the influences of suggestion and persuasion that are written into our social fabric.

We are not each other's guru. And we need normal appreciation, normal encouragement, normal tenderness, and normal special affection. We *need* these things. Our whole human organism needs them. We are not saints, we are not angels; we are embryonic souls immersed in a badly educated body being pulled along by a love-starved lonely horse called the emotions.

In a sense, then, everything that popular psychology tells us about happiness is both true and untrue at the same time. We yearn for success, beauty, material security, recognition, sexual passion, and we each, depending on our type and subjectivity, imagine that one or more of these goals will bring us happiness. The life and culture around us strengthens this belief. And there is truth in this belief. We do need these things. *But in themselves they do not bring happiness.* This is what is not understood by "life"—and it has never been understood, whether that "life" is the society of a modern world or medieval Christendom or ancient India or the great civilizations of ancient China, Egypt, or Babylon. The history that we know shows us few examples of civilizations in which, for any significant duration, the forces favoring inner human development took greater place than the forces leading to conflict, isolation, and barbarism. Perhaps we really do not know how to look at history and at other cultures, but to the extent that we can study them with some degree of impartiality, we see crime, war, brutality, and avarice far outweighing the pursuit of knowledge, artistic truth, religious values, and human compassion.

The Long Work of Love

A man and a woman working at love are always, whether they call it this or not, working to free themselves from attachment to the illusions of "life," while at the same time helping each other to answer the normal needs of the embodied human self. The struggle of love is the struggle against making the other into the "world," compelling the other to give what the "world" or "life" promises but can never really give: absolute safety, unearned loyalty and fidelity, fantastical power, ever-ready pleasure. . . . If "life itself" cannot give these things—and, in the deeper meaning of them, it cannot—then we have no right to try to get them from the other. I have no right to make the other into "life itself." How much of the disappointment with love that men and women now feel in our culture is actually a displaced but unrecognized disappointment with "life itself"!

Wisdom teaches that what we erroneously seek from the "world" is to be found only through the process that opens us to another level of life within ourselves. It is that life, we are told, that can give us what we mistakenly seek outside ourselves. It is "life within life" that can give what "life itself" cannot. And it is a glimpse of that life within life that we sometimes touch when we are in love, when we experience what Stendhal called "the passions which make for deeper joy."

Being in love, we do not strain for beauty, for power, recognition, safety, health. Being in love, we are for a moment, and up to a point, free from the influences of "life itself." Being in love, we touch complete devotion to another, and in that devotion we experience something of our truer self. Being in love, we live beyond paradox. Love brings opposites together—that is its very definition. In the universe, in nature and between people and within ourselves, love is the force that brings disparate and separate realities toward each other into fusion and mutuality.

Being in love, we find ourselves in the moment we find the other; in love, we touch freedom in the moment we serve another; in love, we touch intelligence and clarity in the moment we are given to let go of thought and cleverness; in love, we become strong and safe in the moment we are given to let go of our last pieces of armor and, in an instant and for an instant, we become completely vulnerable. As was said of Baucis and Philemon: "It made no difference in that house whether you asked for master or servant."

"Life itself" cannot understand these things. In "life itself" we live the illusion of strength, for example, and cannot see that it is weakness to be half-vulnerable, to fear and protect our inner feeling with another feeling that lives and breathes only anxiety. "Life itself" cannot open its doors to the "gods," because it cannot understand the strength of love, the safety of love, the freedom of sustained love. And so it immediately strives to make love into something it can understand. This is the challenge of living together. Being in love is one thing; now we must bring what we have tasted into the arena of "life itself." It is now that the long work begins.

The long work begins. Being in love shows us the power of a life within life. That is, it shows us that there is something beyond the influences of ordinary life in the world. It is here that wisdom teaches mankind to search within. Here wisdom instructs us: what we touch in love is like a sign, evidence that we are meant for quite another destiny than what the world around us can give. This other destiny involves the cultivation—the insemination—of a new life within ourselves. Like every embryo, this new life must be cared for and nourished.

The work of love begins. In the midst of life, with all its needs and demands, with all its compromises and details, with all the forces and energies that the gods and devils have thrown upon this plane of being called human life, in the midst of this ever-surging flood of "life itself," mankind is called—two by two, as is suggested in the myth of Noah—to maintain the human reflection of divinity in a world overwhelmed by violence, confusion, and illusion.

Part 2

THE WISDOM
OF LOVE

Chapter Eight

INTENTIONAL LOVE

We have been speaking of "the teachings of wisdom" and we have been trying to see the work of love in the light of these teachings. We have been trying to understand the work of love as the task of supporting each other's search for the life of meaning that wisdom tells us is possible and necessary for humanity.

The flash and glory of falling in love can awaken us, body and soul, to a great unknown within ourselves. But when we live together and face the day-to-day details of life, the continual pressures and complications, the fears and resentments, the disappointments and the strangely hollow triumphs, the *everydayness* of it all, the physical, emotional, and mental labyrinth of "life itself," how can we go on loving each other in a way that is more than only a yearning for another beginning? Another beginning of love, a beginning that, like all human processes, must inevitably come to a crossroads where something intentional and conscious is needed. To be "romantic," in the derogatory sense of the word, is to turn away again and again from the crossroads of the process of love, the place where what is automatically given to us by nature must be joined by something intentional from ourselves. To be romantic, in the derogatory sense, is to yearn only for automatic love. But the work of love begins where automatic love ends.

The wisdom teachings do not speak much of automatic love, or about what we nowadays call "relationships." This is so much so that one might even wonder if men and women of other cultures and worlds experienced anything like the difficulties and rewards that are part of intimate relationships in our culture. In fact, it is probably true that in our industrial and postindustrial society, with all the social changes that have been wrought by technology, the psychological demands of living together are startlingly different in many respects.

But that is not the main point. The point is that when the traditions of wisdom speak about love, they are speaking almost without exception of love that is intentional, love "at the crossroads" and beyond. Confusion enters in mainly because the love spoken of by wisdom is mistakenly viewed as existing on the same level as automatic love. It is a serious error to confuse the kind of love that is given to us by nature with the kind of love we must work for. And, of course, we will never even imagine the work of love if we assume that the higher forms of love are on the same level as the love that is given to us automatically.

We need to look in a new way at what wisdom tells us about love. It is possible, and necessary, to look at the wisdom of love while at the same time inwardly renouncing our usual assumption that these ideas point to something we can do or easily have. We can look at these teachings in a way that returns them to their proper place as *ideals*, not as facts about ourselves. The inspiration they bring can nourish our wish to work for them in the midst of our actual lives, rather than fill us with the fantasy that we are already able to live them. The ideas about love that have been given to mankind through the ages can inform and intensify our metaphysical aspiration and thereby sensitize us to the struggle that will make us human.

Christianity

We can begin this brief survey of the wisdom of love by turning to the expressions that have most powerfully affected our culture and which continue to offer hope in a darkening world. What do these words of the New Testament say to men and women trying to love each other in this present era, this so-called "postmodern world"?

> Ye have heard that it hath been said, Thou shalt love thy neighbor, and hate thine enemy.
> But I say unto you, Love your enemies, bless them that curse you, do good to them that hate

you, and pray for them which despitefully use you, and persecute you . . .

For if ye love them which love you, what reward have ye? do not even the publicans the same?

And if ye salute your brethren only, what do ye more than others? do not even the publicans so?

(Matthew 5:43–47)

Little children, yet a little while I am with you. Ye shall seek me: and as I said unto the Jews, Whither I go, ye cannot come; so now I say unto you.

A new commandment I give unto you, That ye love one another; as I have loved you, that ye also love one another.

(John 13:33–34)

Beloved, let us love one another: for love is of God; and every one that loveth is born of God, and knoweth God.

He that loveth not knoweth not God; for God is love.

(I John 4:7–8)

The New Testament teaching about love centers around the Greek word *agape*. *Agape* is the love that descends upon human beings from God, or from a higher state of being. As such, it is usually distinguished from ordinary human love, which is rooted in incompleteness and desire. *Agape* is the love that pours out from fullness; ordinary human love, so goes the conventional analysis, arises out of lack and the sense of personal need, which we can take to include sexual need, or social/psychologically conditioned need, which itself sometimes includes elements of the moral strictures and demands that are part of the social fabric.

Understood in this general way, *agape* seems to be an ideal that is out of human reach. Or, alternatively, if it is understood to be within human reach, it is only because the idea of *agape* is surreptitiously reduced to something within the range of ordinary human love. Understood in the first way, that is, as a power of love that is out of the reach of ordinary men and women, it cannot really enter into our day-to-day lives even as an ideal. For what is the meaning of an ideal that no one can possibly ever attain? Understood in the second way, as akin to ordinary human love, it becomes an idea that simply masks our actual condition of emotional neurosis. When the ideal of *agape* is surreptitiously reduced to automatic human love, it even makes life more, rather than less, difficult. In its name, it is not uncommon for violence and crime to flourish. Under the name of Christian love, wars and inquisitions have brought immeasurable pain to mankind.

But the Christian ideal of love can have immense practical meaning. Are there steps toward it that we can take? Can this ideal help us to understand more clearly the practical effort of what we have called intermediate love between two people?

The chief element of *agape* that distinguishes it from ordinary human love is that it is not automatic. *Agape* is nothing if it is not intentional. It is a love that can be commanded; that means, it does not depend entirely on a wave of emotion over which an individual has no control.

At the same time, it is not something we can will in our usual psychological state. So, the mystery is there: at its deepest reaches, *agape* is not subject to our will in any way. Yet, it is commanded of us. It is not something we can *do*. Yet, wisdom tells us we must love.

What is the reconciliation of these two contradictory aspects of the idea of *agape?*

The Commandment to Love

We can find our way with this question with the help of the great nineteenth-century Danish thinker Søren Kierkegaard:

> And when the eternal says, "You shall love," it becomes the eternal's responsibility to make sure that it can be done.*

That is, *agape* is not within our power, but it is a power that we can be given, a capacity that a human being can receive. What seems to have been generally forgotten about this commandment to love is that in order to obey it a man or woman must be able—not directly to love, but to open him- or herself to the transcendent power that

---

* Søren Kierkegaard, *Works of Love*, trans. Howard and Edna Hong, New York: Harper Torchbooks, 1962, p. 55.

draws all conscious beings toward each other through drawing them toward the fundamental source of the universe itself. Such is the basic metaphysics of Christian love. But what is also forgotten is that this ableness to open to the power of *agape* is not itself given outright. It must be worked for, struggled for. This struggle is another name for what we call the search for meaning. And it is this search for meaning, which now we see implies the capacity to love as God loves, which can bring two people together for mutual help. Perhaps two people cannot will the transcendent feeling of Christian love; they—we—are not developed to that point. But they can will, that is, choose, to try to support each other's struggle to move toward that capacity in ourselves. Such a choice, from moment to moment, is not *agape*, but it echoes *agape*; it has about it, to use the imagery of the Islamic mystics, the "perfume" of conscious love.

Listen again to Kierkegaard. The power intentionally to love another human being, Kierkegaard tells us, comes to us only as a *result* of our ability to open to the Higher (the eternal or God) within and above:

The matter is quite simple. Man shall begin by loving the unseen God, for thereby he himself shall learn what it is to love. But the fact that he really loves the unseen shall be indicated precisely by this, that he loves the brother he sees. The more he loves the unseen, the more he will love the men he sees. It is not the opposite, that the more he rejects those he sees, the more he loves the unseen, for when this is the case, God is changed into an unreal something, a fancy. Such a thing can occur only to a hypocrite or to a deceiver in order to find an escape, or to one who misrepresents God, as if God were grasping for his own interest and his being loved, rather than that the holy God is gracious and therefore always points away from himself, saying, as it were, "If you wish to love me, love the men you see. Whatever you do for them you do for me." God is too exalted to be able to accept a man's love directly, to say nothing of being able to find pleasure in what pleases a fanatic. . . . God demands nothing for himself, although he demands everything from you. . . .*

* Works of Love, pp. 158–59.

Kierkegaard is speaking of a wholeness of intention within the self, an intention that is directed simultaneously toward God and toward one's neighbor, an intention of the heart and soul open simultaneously toward what is deeply within oneself and toward the actual human being before one. It is a grave error, says Kierkegaard, to imagine one can love another person intentionally without at the same time—and *more fundamentally*—loving the Highest within oneself and above oneself.

Chapter Nine

ETHICS AS LOVE

It is not often enough noted that this capacity to love intentionally, with the whole of one's being, is what makes a human being *godlike*. If man is made in the image of God—and this is the view of both the Judaic and the Christian teaching—it means he is built to be capable of love. "God is love."

Judaism

Here one sees the answer to the riddle of the serpent in paradise—a story that has so much to teach us about the meaning of love between a man and woman. The serpent tempts Eve in the painfully mysterious moment when Eve says to the serpent:

> But of the fruit of the tree which is in the midst of the garden, God hath said, Ye shall not eat of it, neither shall ye touch it, lest ye die.
>
> And the serpent said unto the woman, Ye shall not surely die:
>
> For God doth know that in the day ye eat thereof, then your eyes shall be opened, and ye shall be as gods, knowing good and evil.
>
> And when the woman saw that the tree was good for food, and that it was pleasant to the eyes, and a tree to be desired to make one wise, she took of the fruit thereof, and did eat, and gave also unto her husband with her; and he did eat.
>
> (Genesis 3:3–6)

"Ye shall be as gods": the word "gods," *elohim,* here does not necessarily refer to the Highest. "Ye shall be as gods" may refer to princes, rulers —even the rulers of the world. The word *elohim* does not *necessarily* in every context refer to God the creator and father. In any case, for us the point to emphasize in this story is that the apple is *pleasant to the eyes.* It *looks* good. It appears good. It seems to make one wise. In this story of the fall, humanity falls into the world of appearances, a world in which one lives from only the surface of the self; a world in which one desires and takes and thinks and prefers, liking and disliking. This is not godlike; it is only the "godlikeness" of the ego.

Yet mankind is destined and built for godlikeness. But this is a state that comes from the capacity and the action of love. As it is said in countless places in the Old Testament, but most notably in Deuteronomy 6:

Hear, O Israel: The Lord our God is one Lord:

And thou shalt love the Lord thy God with all thine heart, and with all thy soul, and with all thy might.

(Deuteronomy 6:4–5)

Thou shalt love with the whole of one's being, not "like" or "dislike" from the surface. Deuteronomy 6 is the answer to Genesis 3. The human being as the image and likeness of God is the human being who can love with the whole of the self—mind, heart, body, "with all thine heart, and with all thy soul, and with all thy might." And it is first and foremost God who is to be loved with this wholeness of being, intention, and understanding.

The Love That Makes Us Human

The sequence and structure of the Ten Commandments now enter to inform us that ethics, the realm of relationships between human beings, is derivative from man's capacity to love the eternal—exactly as Kierkegaard and others have indicated. The first commandments are precisely about humanity's relationship to the Highest; only after this is established are the commandments given that pertain to the "horizontal" aspect of life, the cultivation of relationships and actions with people, individually and collectively. Love for the other is at root derivative, or, to be precise, a *result* of love for the holy God within and above.

The first five commandments concern man's relationship to God and may be read as explanations of the fundamental commandment of Deuteronomy 6, "Thou shalt love the Lord thy God with all thine heart, and with all thy soul, and with all thy might." The Ten Commandments are given in Deuteronomy just before this fundamental commandment of love; in their more often cited, and more compact, version they are also given in the book of Exodus.

> And God spake all these words, saying,
> *I am the Lord thy God, which have brought thee out of the land of Egypt, out of the house of bondage.*
> (Exodus 20:1–2; italics added)

This bondage is not only literal; inwardly, it is the bondage, the slavery to the tyrant within the self, the "pharaoh" of the false selfhood which tyrannizes the life within.

Thou shalt have no other gods before me.
(Exodus 20:3; italics added)

Turn for help and understanding and well-being and for all else that you truly need, to the source of all being and goodness. Do not turn to what is less than God for that which can be given only by God —within and above. This corresponds to the dictum of Jesus:

For all these things do the nations of the world seek after: and your Father knoweth that ye have need of these things.

But rather seek ye the kingdom of God; and all these things shall be added unto you.
(Luke 12:30–31)

There are countless views, objects of desire, fears, pleasures and needs, normal and abnormal, which rule our mind and heart; which usurp the place of God. These, inwardly, are the "idols" of the Abrahamic religions—Judaism, Christianity, and Islam. One of the chief idols, as St. Augustine so movingly describes in the *Confessions,* can be a certain kind of love for another human being. There, Augustine speaks of the shock of the sudden death of his dearest friend when they were both in the prime of their youth. He realizes that he "had loved him as though he would never die."

> Blessed are those who love you, O God, and love their friends in you. . . . They alone will never lose those who are dear to them, for they love them in one who is never lost, in God, our God who made heaven and earth and fills them with his presence, because by filling them he made them.*

It was St. Augustine's life-transforming discovery that we cannot truly love another without loving, or *seeking to love,* that force or Being that creates us, that is, that *makes us human.*

---

* St. Augustine, *Confessions,* trans., R. S. Pine-Coffin, Baltimore: Penguin Books, 1961, pp. 79–80.

Stone Figures

In what now follows in Exodus, we are told of the inevitable consequences of turning for meaning and happiness to objects of desire or thought which we invent or project from the surface of ourselves, from our ego. The powerful Hebraic strictures against idolatry are not to be interpreted only as applying to some melodramatic fantastical picture we may have of so-called "primitive" or "heathen" peoples worshiping stone figures as though the stones were God. We may grasp these powerful biblical interdictions in a far more inward manner, as applying to the rigid "stone figures" we carve out within our own psychological world of thought, sensation, and emotion. What in fact do we turn to for help and for meaning, within ourselves? The Hebraic vision, and in this it echoes every great spiritual tradition in history, is that these interior idols *have no real power* to make us fully human. They are, as it were, "local deities"; they bring the *appearance* of power, knowledge, and meaning—but it is not real, it does not withstand the forces of life and death; they do not open us to our neighbor. They are false gods—false *elohim* or rulers.

> Thou shalt not make unto thee any graven image, or any likeness of any thing that is in heaven above, or that is in the earth beneath, or that is in the water under the earth:
>
> Thou shalt not bow down thyself to them, nor serve them: for I the Lord thy God am a jealous God, visiting the iniquity of the fathers upon the children unto the third and fourth generation of them that hate me;
>
> And showing mercy unto thousands of them that love me, and keep my commandments.
>
> (Exodus 20:4–6)

The Basis of Morality

There follows the commandment that forbids taking the name of God in vain, which in its more inner meaning is also a warning against mixing up levels of reality in one's feelings and understanding. The fifth commandment concerns the sabbath, the need for stillness and the intentional consecration of time to God within and above. The sabbath commandment is one of the few direct indications in the Old Testament of what was doubtless part of the science or method of the Hebraic religion, a practice the modern world is now beginning to remember under the name of meditation and contemplation. The sabbath commandment, that is, points to the possible existence in the ancient Hebraic tradition of the kind of spiritual science that we know was preserved in the religions of the East under the name of yoga in its various forms.

The strong traditions of family life and ritual in the Judaic religion revolve around the obligation of man and wife to support each other's religious practice—not unlike what we have been calling "intermediate love." The making of a home, the creation of adequate material security, the guidance in fulfilling equal, but different roles with respect to children, health, and the atmosphere of tenderness —all this is often spoken of not as practices advised for their own sake or solely for peace of mind, but as mutual help given by a man and woman to make them freer to search for God.

Only after these commandments concerning an

individual's relationship to God are we given the commandments dealing with the relationship to other human beings.

> Honour thy father and thy mother: that thy days may be long upon the land which the Lord thy God giveth thee.
>
> Thou shalt not kill.
>
> Thou shalt not commit adultery.
>
> Thou shalt not steal.
>
> Thou shalt not bear false witness against thy neighbour.
>
> Thou shalt not covet thy neighbour's house, thou shalt not covet thy neighbour's wife, nor his manservant, nor his maidservant, nor his ox, nor his ass, nor any thing that is thy neighbour's.
>
> And all the people saw the thunderings, and the lightnings, and the noise of the trumpet, and the mountain smoking: and when the people saw it, they removed, and stood afar off.
>
> (Exodus 20:12–18)

These commandments are the basis of all morality, Eastern as well as Western. In no civilization and in no tradition of spiritual wisdom do we find any significant departure from the essence of these commandments dealing with man's relationships and behavior vis-à-vis his neighbor. They are given to be practiced and cultivated, even against all one's impulses and desires. No great teaching that has formed the core of any authentic human social order has ever dreamed that all human beings would behave spontaneously from their hearts according to these commandments. Obviously, for most of us, these commandments are ideals by which we measure our possible moral development and our actual moral incapacity.

Yet they may also be understood as portrayals of the heart and behavior of more developed men and women. Intermediate love is the support two people can give each other in their search and struggle to become men and women of *moral power.**

---

* G. I. Gurdjieff, *Views from the Real World*, New York: Arkana, 1984, pp. 159–63.

Intermediate Ethics

In this sense, we can speak also of *intermediate ethics,* intermediate morality. There exists as an ideal and as a standard against which we measure ourselves, the ancient teachings of the great traditions: the rules of conduct, the laws of behavior, many of which in their endless application to the details of life must be enforced by coercion and legality merely in order to keep human society intact. But at their root, these moral laws represent the spontaneous behavior of men and women of great inner development, men and women in whom the depth of conscience is active. The Ten Commandments and their equivalent in other spiritual teachings of the world are the natural expression of the essence of the divine/human consciousness. To be open to the great life within us is to be open to the life all around us, especially human life. We—the masses of men and women trying to live a decent life—we in our everyday lives wish to, and outwardly most often do, obey the laws that spring from the dictates of the depths of human conscience, we obey the laws and principles that are the traces of divine perception within exceptional human beings. We obey them not so much out of inclination but out of duty. Much inside us resists these commandments, much resists the duty that our religiously based laws of morality present to us. As the philosophers Kant and Hegel, and after them Nietzsche, put it: in us, as we are, "Thou shalt" constantly wars with "I wish." But in the human being that we are called to become through inner struggle, "Thou shalt" begins to converge with "I wish." An individual deep, spontaneous impulse converges and, ultimately, fuses with the commandments of the law. Thus St. Augustine: "Love God and do what you wish."

But first one must love God. And to love God is not a simple thing, it is not an automatic capacity of human beings. It must be worked for; and, as an ideal, a goal, it is one of the chief ways of expressing the possible inner development of a human being.

The teachings of wisdom speak of a discipline and a struggle that leads toward this capacity to love God with all one's being. This struggle also has its rules and laws and its *ethics*. There exists the *ethics of the search*. These are the principles and laws and obligations through which individuals can help each other or at least support each other in the movement toward the capacity to love God, or, simply, the capacity to *be*. This *ethics of the search* cannot necessarily be written down in a book or text. The search, or—to use a great word from the traditions—the *Way* embodies principles that must continually be discovered through one's own dynamic struggle. But the sensitivity of intermediate love, the wish for another's growth, can be allowed to emerge naturally from one's own perception of the human situation in oneself, a perception which opens us to the same need and wish in the other. In a like manner, the appearance of the wish to struggle with oneself in another can spontaneously open our hearts to the other in a way that no automatic impulses of love and affection can equal. Thus intermediate ethics is born from intermediate love, just as in the great world of wisdom and being, the great commandments of duty are in their origin born from the mystic contact with God above and within.

We have heard about love from the teachings of Jesus and from the laws of Moses. What necessary truths about intentional love can we learn from other traditions or individuals?

Chapter Ten

TWO POETS:
RUMI AND RILKE

Consider the poetry of the thirteenth-century
Persian Jalal al-Din Rumi, a master of
the inner search as it exists within the traditions of Islam, and the source of an extraordinary wealth of articulated, poetic vision, as
precise as it is passionate, about the meaning of
conscious human love. We do not know exactly
how he created his poetry. Some say he
considered it merely a secondary, and perhaps
even unimportant, expression of his experience of

the states of inner freedom. In any case, recent renderings of Rumi into contemporary English help us see that the common human experience of the state of being in love can actually, tangibly, echo the even more exalted condition of love for the God above and within. This poetry does more than treat sexual love as a literary metaphor for divine love. It shows us that the tender passions and sufferings of the love that rises by itself between men and women is like a foretaste, an arrow pointing to the path of conscious joy and union that is traditionally spoken of as the "merging with God."

The Opening of Intentional Love

Through the use of what we in fact know of human passion, the startlingly beautiful poetry of Rumi communicates precise impressions of the search for inner freedom. In this poetry, we see knowledge offered to the mind and the feelings simultaneously. Through the language of automatic love, Rumi instructs us about the nature of intentional love.

Finally, and most important for our present concern, this poetry—like much spiritual love poetry—shows us that intentional love is an intentional allowing, not a tense imposition of the mind upon the body or the heart. Unlike the intentions of the ego, intentional love is not a contraction. It is a "mystery in broad daylight," a weakness that is a strength. It is the "death" of the mind—that is, the dominant mind of egoism; and the birth of reason, that is, the wordless vision of reality and oneself.

> *After being with me one*
> *whole night,*
> *you ask how I live when you're*
> *not here.*
> *Badly, frantically, like a fish*
> *trying to breathe*
> *dry sand. You weep and say,*
> But you choose that.*

* John Moyne and Coleman Barks, *Unseen Rain: Quatrains of Rumi*, Putney, Vermont: Threshold Books, 1986, p. 25.

"You" are the God within and above, and the way to this God. *"You"* are human joy and meaning. And again and again I turn away from *"You."* We turn away from what we love and from what loves our inner nature. This is a precise impression. All who search will verify this experience. Intermediate love between people can help us turn our energies again and again to facing this truth about ourselves. Out of this confrontation there arises a profound longing, a sense of lack that can become the strongest force in human life, that is like the passionate longing a man and woman can feel for each other. In fact, in that longing of human passion, there is the resonance and echo of the longing for inward contact with the energy that makes us human—that is, God the Creator.

> *There's no love in me without your being,*
> *no breath without that. I once thought*
> *I could give up this longing, then*
> > *thought again,*
> But I couldn't continue being
> > human.*

* *Unseen Rain*, p. 76.

Dissolver of sugar, dissolve me,
if this is the time.
Do it gently with a touch of hand,
    or a look.
Every morning I wait at dawn. That's
    when it's happened before.
Or do it suddenly like an execution.
    How else
can I get ready for death?
You breathe without a body like a spark.
You grieve, and I begin to feel lighter.
You keep me away with your arm,
*but the keeping away is pulling me in.**

Human lovers who resonate with such teachings can understand something new about the days and years together of men and women who are working to love each other. Every serious man or woman can understand that no human being can or ought to still the longing that Rumi speaks of. No person can ever be God for another. And the question arises: How much of what we call love is the

* John Moyne and Coleman Barks, trans., *Open Secret: Versions of Rumi*, Putney, Vermont: Threshold Books, 1984, p. 70.

attempt to be God for another or to make the other into God for ourselves? Intermediate love understands this. Mysteriously, the mutual understanding of this fundamental truth creates a bond between people unlike any other bond. It fuses people together far more than the dreams of romance could ever imagine. We very much need reports from men and women who have tried to love in this way. I think we need such reports—perhaps in whispers—far more than we need our culture's continual talking about the automatisms of love.

Rilke: The Apprenticeship of Love

One such "report"—which has had great influence on people who become aware of it—comes from the great modern poet Rainer Maria Rilke. When Rilke refers to "young people," of course, what he is saying is true of all of us, at any age.

> There is scarcely anything more difficult than to love one another. That it is work, day labor, day labor, God knows there is no other word for

it. And look, added to this is the fact that young people are not prepared for such difficult loving; for convention has tried to make this most complicated and ultimate relationship into something easy and frivolous, has given it the appearance of everyone's being able to do it. It is not so. Love is something difficult and it is more difficult than other things because in other conflicts nature herself enjoins men to collect themselves, to take themselves firmly in hand with all their strength, while in the heightening of love the impulse is to give oneself wholly away. But just think, can that be anything beautiful, to give oneself away not as something whole and ordered, but haphazard rather, bit by bit, as it comes? Can such giving away, that looks so like a throwing away and dismemberment, be anything good, can it be happiness, joy, progress? No, it cannot. . . . When you give someone flowers, you arrange them beforehand, don't you? But young people who love each other fling themselves to each other in the impatience and haste of their passion, and they don't notice at all what a lack of mutual esteem lies in this disordered giving of themselves; they notice it with astonishment and indignation only from the dissension that arises between them out of all this disorder. And once there is disunity between them, the confusion grows with every day; neither of the two has anything unbroken, pure, and unspoiled about him any longer, and amid the disconsolateness of a break they try to hold fast to the semblance of their happiness (for all that was really supposed to be for the sake of happiness). Alas, they are scarcely able to recall any more what they meant by happiness. In his uncertainty each becomes more and more unjust toward the other; they who wanted to do each other good are now handling one another in an imperious and intolerant manner, and in the struggle somehow to get out of their untenable and unbearable state of confusion, they commit the greatest fault that can happen to human relationships: they become impatient. They hurry to a conclusion; to come, as they believe, to a final decision, they try once and for all to establish their relationship, whose surprising changes have frightened them, in order to remain the same now and *forever* (as they say). That is only the last error in this long chain of errings linked fast to one another. . . .

And now Rilke gives us a glimpse of what love can be as a result of work:

> Self-transformation is precisely what life is, and human relationships, which are an extract of life, are the most changeable of all, rising and falling from minute to minute, and lovers are those in whose relationship and contact no one moment resembles another. . . .
>
> There are such relationships, which must be a very great, almost unbearable happiness, but they can occur only between very rich natures and between those who, each for himself, are richly ordered and composed; they can unite only two wide, deep, individual worlds. —Young people —it is obvious—cannot achieve such a relationship, but they can, if they understand their life properly, grow up slowly to such happiness and prepare themselves for it. They must not forget, when they love, that they are beginners, bunglers of life, apprentices in love—must *learn* love, and that (like *all* learning) wants peace, patience, and composure!
>
> . . . Like so much else, people have also misunderstood the place of love in life, they have

made it into play and pleasure because they thought that play and pleasure were more blissful than work; but there is nothing happier than work, and love, just because it is the extreme happiness, can be nothing else but work. —So whoever loves must try to act as if he had a great work; he must be much alone and go into himself and collect himself and hold fast to himself; he must work; he must become something!

For believe me, the more one is, the richer is all that one experiences. And whoever wants to have a deep love in his life must collect and save for it and gather honey.

Here, it is clear, Rilke is speaking not only of how two people can nourish each other's inner life, but of the capacity to love as being a result of the inner search. One level of intentional love is required from us from the very beginning. Another level represents a capacity of a more developed man or woman.

Whoever looks seriously at it finds that neither for death, which is difficult, nor for difficult love has any explanation, any solution, any hint or way yet been discerned; and for these two problems that we carry wrapped up and hand on without opening, it will not be possible to discover any general rule resting in agreement. But in the same measure in which we begin as individuals to put life to the test, we shall, being individuals, meet these great things at closer range. The demands which the difficult work of love makes upon our development are more than life-size, and as beginners we are not up to them. But if we nevertheless hold out and take this love upon us as burden and apprenticeship, instead of losing ourselves in all the light and frivolous play, behind which people have hidden from the most earnest earnestness of their existence—then a little progress and an alleviation will perhaps be perceptible to those who come long after us; that would be much.

Finally, the demand to love—sexually and otherwise, along with the possibility of loving consciously—resides in our essence as human beings, as links in the chain of generations. We cannot help but pass this mystery on to those who come after us.

Do not be bewildered by the surfaces; in the depths all becomes law. And those who live the secret wrong and badly (and they are very many), lose it only for themselves and still hand it on, like a sealed letter, without knowing it.*

Chapter Eleven

IMPERSONAL LOVE

Turning now to the vastness of India, we encounter an idea that, no less than the Christian *agape*, echoes the mystery of a love at once passionate and impartial. The word *bhakti* in the traditions of India means devotion, surrender of one's multiple personal desires to the single will of the divine. But such one-pointed conscious surrender cannot take place without a long and difficult struggle against the ego's tendencies toward either sentimentality, anxiety, sensory distractions, or cold, arrogant logic. The word *bhakti* thus refers to a capacity of devotion that rises far above the emotional tension which afflicts so much of our common experience of love. Like *agape*, *bhakti* develops in the individual through the struggle to free oneself from entrapment in the personal emotions.

The Emotional Unknown

Like Christian love, *bhakti* points to a new quality of feeling within the psyche, a quality only rarely approached in the course of ordinary life. One sometimes glimpses this quality of feeling in tragic or joyous moments of life, but such experiences are afterward usually interpreted only as intensifications of our more familiar kinds of emotional experience. We fail to realize that in certain rare moments—where, for example, we risk everything to help another, or where we come face to face with death—we touch a completely unknown capacity of love within us.

The idea of a great emotional unknown is as important as the more familiar idea of higher knowledge or higher powers of thought. When the possibilities of human growth and development are envisaged in literature and philosophy—in science fiction, for example—it usually involves the development of the mind. The possible development of the emotional function is much more difficult to envisage when one is working within the pattern of purely mental or physical development.

Yet the teachings of all religions and spiritual philosophies give us portraits of men and women in whom the emotional function has been highly developed—or, to be more precise, in whom there is active an entirely unknown function of feeling. What are the models of the world's saints and holy men and women, or a figure such as Socrates, if they are not portrayals of the action of the unknown higher emotional functions—what we might also term *impersonal love?* It is no service to us to treat the accounts of this capacity as comparable to our own subjective personal emotions and to regard such capacities, therefore, as attainable by us either without effort or through what we ordinarily understand as effort. The emotional unknown is no less a mystery than the Kantian *noumenon* or the traditional "world beyond the veil." Yet this emotional unknown is at the same time *our possibility*. The teachings of wisdom call us to it.

The *Bhagavad Gita*

Here is an invocation of the meaning of *bhakti* from the *Bhagavad Gita*, India's most widely revered sacred text. Krishna (God) is speaking to the warrior Arjuna, who represents the human being struggling with great intensity along the *Way* of inner transformation.

This particular passage from the *Gita*, with its list of traits that define the nature of *bhakti*, should no doubt be read more than once, and rather slowly, with the reader trying to picture how he or she actually reacts to the situations of life that are evoked here, situations where one is hurt by another or flattered or unjustly accused or ignored or stroked. It is very difficult, perhaps impossible, to bring forth in the imagination these everyday emotions that continually tumble us from happiness to despair and back again, emotions which almost always revolve around love in its various aspects. But if we can try to recall the startling power of even the tiniest slights and fears and unexpected gratifications, or, on the other hand, the unyielding emotional and physical grip of cold resentment, hatred, and contempt, we may glimpse the level of human attainment that is spoken of here under the name of *bhakti.*

Those who have actually tried to live concretely the life of impersonal love, who have tried to regard other men and women as unique manifestations of God—however this God is named—can attest to the immensity of the task, and therefore the level of inner freedom that must be attributed to those who can actually conform their motivations to this ideal.

Here, then, is the *Gita*'s characterization of *bhakti,* or nonegoistic devotion to the divine, and the interior qualities of the man or woman who is capable of practicing such devotion.

Krishna speaks:

Those who set their hearts on me and worship me with unfailing devotion and faith are more established in yoga [spiritual discipline] . . .

Yet hazardous and slow is the path to the Unrevealed, difficult for physical man to tread. But they for whom I am the supreme goal, who do all work renouncing self for me and meditate on me with single-hearted devotion, these I will swiftly rescue from the . . . cycle of birth and death, for their consciousness has entered into me.

And now Krishna speaks of how this inner liberation from the meaningless agitation of illusion is to be sought, taking into account the seeker's capacities and weaknesses:

Still your mind in me, still your intellect in me, and without doubt you will be united with me forever. If you cannot still your mind in me, learn to do so through the regular practice of meditation. If you lack the will for such self-discipline, engage yourself in [service to] my work, for selfless service can lead you at last to complete fulfillment.

But finally, if the individual is unable to practice any of these ways, one last method is left: to act in life without attachment to the results of one's actions, whether they be good or bad.

If you are unable to do even this, surrender yourself to me, disciplining yourself and renouncing
the results of all your actions . . .

And now we are given a portrait of the state of the
self that is brought about by such practices:

That one I love who is incapable of ill will, who
is friendly and compassionate. Living beyond the
reach of *I* and *mine* and of pleasure and pain,
patient, contented, self-controlled, firm in faith,
with all his heart and all his mind given to me—
with such a one I am in love.

Not agitating the world or by it agitated, he
stands above the sway of elation, competition and
fear: he is my beloved.

He is detached, pure, efficient, impartial, never
anxious, selfless in all his undertakings; he is my
devotee, very dear to me.

He is dear to me who runs not after the pleasant
or away from the painful, grieves not, lusts not,
but lets things come and go as they happen.

The devotee who looks upon friend and foe with
equal regard, who is not buoyed up by praise nor
cast down by blame, alike in heat or cold, plea-

sure and pain, free from selfish attachments, the same in honor and dishonor, quiet, ever full, in harmony everywhere, firm in faith—such a one is dear to me.*

What We Know of Impersonal Love

Such passages, and the sacred writings of the world are replete with them, bring us again and again to the need to know realistically what is actually possible for us as we are. If we are sincere, we know that such impersonal nonegoistic love—love that is entirely independent of the mechanisms of the body's likes and dislikes, and the psychological desires and fears that have been conditioned into us from earliest childhood—remains an ideal for us, not an attribute of actual emotional makeup. At the same time, an honest inventory of our own inner lives also shows us that there are moments in our lives when we come close to such love, when we

* *Bhagavad Gita*, trans. by Eknath Easwaran, Petaluma, Calif.: Nilgiri Press, 1985, pp. 162–64.

may actually experience it. In situations of physical danger, for example, it can happen that a man or woman immediately sets aside personal emotions and acts only for the welfare of another. In times of great grief, immediately following the death of a loved one, it often happens that all egoism vanishes, that no trace remains of personal emotions such as anger or resentment or self-pity or any impulse toward personal gain. What then appears, when these personal emotions retreat, is an entirely new and yet strangely familiar quality of feeling. In this state, an individual looks with calm and even acceptance upon everyone who comes his way. It is impossible to be perturbed or "negative," yet this calmness is far from coldness. It is like a smokeless flame, pure light and warmth. In fact, it is surely a taste of the kind of love we hear about in the sacred writings and in the stories of holy men and women.

What we are calling intermediate love is based on the desire to be capable of such love in any situation of life. But intermediate love recognizes that this capacity is difficult to attain and requires a definite and enduring struggle to come toward it. To be toward another person in a way that supports this struggle is the full meaning of intermediate love. To be in this way toward the man or woman with whom we are sharing our life is to approach a transcendent purpose within the sometimes wondrous and sometimes agonizing round of joy and sorrow that makes up all our lives together no matter how they may be judged according to the standards of society.

Is it possible that the notion of marriage as a sacrament is rooted in the need for such intermediate love between two people? That is, that within the spaces, as it were, of a life that brings forth a family and a service to human society, the inner aim of two people together is to witness and support each other's search for that which goes beyond the family and the society?

Concerning the possibility of intentional love and the significance of impersonal emotion, the twentieth-century philosopher and pupil of Gurdjieff, P. D. Ouspensky, offers a vision of considerable power and originality:

> The sign of the growth of the emotions is their liberation from the *personal element* and their transition to higher planes. The liberation from

personal elements enhances the cognitive power of emotions, because the more personal elements there are in an emotion, the more capable it is of leading into delusion. A personal emotion is always *biased*, always *unfair*, if only for the reason that it opposes *itself* to everything else. . . .

Just as it is wrong in relation to oneself to evaluate everything from the point of view of *one emotion*, opposing it to all the rest, so it is wrong in relation to the world and to people to evaluate everything from the point of view of some one accidental "I" of one's own, opposing the self of a given moment to all the rest.

Thus the problem of right emotional knowledge is to *feel* in relation to people and the world *from a point of view other than the personal*. And the wider the circle *for which* a given person feels, the deeper the knowledge which his emotions give. But not all emotions are capable in equal measure of being freed from *self-elements*. There are emotions which by their very nature *divide*, estrange, alienate, make a man feel himself as someone apart, separate; such are hate, fear, jealousy, pride, envy. . . . And there are emotions which *unite*, bring together, make a man feel a part of some large whole; such are love, sympathy, friendship, compassion, love of one's country, love of nature, love of mankind. . . . Emotions of the second order are more easily freed from self-elements than emotions of the first order. Although at the same time there can be quite an *impersonal* pride—pride in some heroic deed performed by *another man*. There may even be an *impersonal envy*, when we envy a man who has conquered himself, conquered his *personal* desire to live, sacrificed himself for something which everybody considers to be *right* and *just* and yet which other people cannot bring themselves to do; dare not even think about *through weakness, through attachment to life*. There may be an *impersonal* hatred—hatred of injustice, violence, anger against stupidity, against dullness; aversion to foulness, to hypocrisy. These feelings undoubtedly lift up and purify man's soul and help him to *see* things which he would not otherwise see.

Christ driving the money changers out of the temple or expressing his opinion of the Pharisees was not at all meek or mild. And there are cases where meekness and mildness are not a virtue at all. Emotions of love, sympathy, pity are very easily transformed into sentimentality, into weakness. . . . The difficulty of dividing emotions into categories is increased by the fact that all emotions of the higher order, without exception, can also be personal, and then their effect is no different from that of the other category.*

* P. D. Ouspensky, *Tertium Organum*, New York: Alfred A. Knopf, 1981, pp. 185–87.

Chapter Twelve

THE PRACTICE OF LOVE

When we speak of intermediate love, we are speaking of a love that is neither the passion of personal desire nor the pure, impersonal love spoken of in the spiritual traditions of the world as God's love for man, or as the love that emanates from the embodiment of God—the Christian savior, the Hebraic prophet or *zaddik*, the Sufi sheikh, the Hindu guru, the Buddhist *bodhisattva*. Intermediate love is a love that is possible for ordinary men and women such as ourselves, but which is yet a step beyond the passions given to us by our human biological heredity and by the mechanisms of custom and culture. Such a love is more intentional than passion, but not yet the force of conscious giving and devotion that is *agape* or *bhakti*. The thesis of this book is that the ideal of sustained love between a man and a woman calls us to practice a love that is neither purely passionate nor purely spiritual.

Or shall we say that intermediate love partakes of *both* the personal and the impersonal? In fact, the *practical* teachings of wisdom point to a love that is just that—a love that carries both the personal intensity of subjective desire *and* the selfless wish for another's well-being.

Buddhism

The Buddhist tradition, for example, urges its followers to regard all human beings as individuals striving for enlightenment. Although the ethics of Buddhism touches on all aspects of life—the physical, personal, and familial—yet at the same time the Buddhist is urged to treat others *primarily* as yearning, consciously or not, toward the inner freedom of *nirvana*, and to regard the suffering of all beings as due fundamentally to their deep ignorance of the nature of the self. While loving and caring for one's own, one's mate or son or daughter or mother or father, the Buddhist seeks to see others as fundamentally in need of metaphysical help.

No doubt, such an ideal of caring for others both as individuals with physical and emotional needs *and* as individuals in need of self-understanding was practiced most intensively among the community of pupils of the teaching, the community known as the *sangha*. To practice such dual love requires that a man or woman understand this dual aspect of human life within him- or herself. Within oneself are both the desires that are a part of having a body and a social "self" *and* the strivings that are evidence of the Buddha or awakened nature within. Those most acutely aware of this whole aspect of human life are the men and women who, in the deeper sense of the term, form the "assembly" of seekers, those who have "entered the stream" of the inner search. Yet Buddhism calls men and women to regard *all* beings as—in some profound sense—seekers of the truth.

How did the members of the earliest Buddhist community strive to work with each other? What kind of care for the other was set as an ideal for these individuals who were living and searching together—with all the emotional demands and contradictions that inevitably test close human relationships? The glorious ideal of impersonal love for all beings—how was it brought to bear on the feelings and reactions of people who were not distant strangers, unknown "neighbors," but people who rubbed against each other every day? It is very possible that it is in such a context—throughout the world, wherever spiritual communities arise—that the practice of intermediate love is born and developed and then passes, up to a point, into the larger world of individual men and women in their ordinary lives together.

Dating from perhaps over five hundred years before the birth of Christ, the following fragment of Buddhist scripture expresses the ideal, not only of impersonal love but of the *striving* for impersonal love, the *work* that leads to selfless love:

Let no one deceive another or despise any
being in any state, let none by anger or
hatred wish harm to another.

As a mother watches over her child,
willing to risk her own life to protect
her only child, so with a boundless
heart should one cherish all living
beings, suffusing the whole world with
unobstructed loving-kindness.

Standing or walking, sitting or lying
down, during all one's waking hours,
may one remain mindful of this heart
and this way of living that is the best
in the world.

Unattached to speculations, views and sense
desires, with clear vision, such a person
will never be reborn in the cycles of
suffering.*

The context of such counsels is that of struggle, inner search—or what the Buddhists call "recollection." "Standing or walking, sitting or lying

---

* Samuel Bercholz and Sherab Chödzih Kohn, eds., *Entering the Stream*, Boston: Shambhala, 1993, p. 142.

down"—that is, at all times in one's waking life—
the individual is asked to be mindful of the capacity within oneself to wish for the good of all people and all that lives. But such constant loving
mindfulness is not automatic. Such a loving will
must be worked for—no matter what one hears
about "non-effort."

Our point here, however, does not so much
concern the life of the community of seekers—that
is, monastic conditions of life and association. The
question is: Can this ideal be brought in some measure into the life of individual men and women
working to love each other in their lives together?
That has been the subject of this book. And the
answer to this question lies, surely, in one's wish to
honor the other's search for inner freedom and
truth, and in the practical understanding of how
this search may be supported amid the details of
living, amid the exquisite passion and tenderness,
the joys and sorrows and fears, the tensions, the
work and play, the distractions and pressures, the
boredom and excitement of the round of ordinary
life in this ordinary world which we all inhabit.

Between Time and Eternity

In fact, our own Western traditions have a specific characterization of this intermediate love, this love that is both desire and desirelessness at the same time, this love that is the possibility of human beings who are in their essence both of the world and beyond the world at the same time. What is this love that corresponds to the two natures of man—this potential synthesis of time and eternity?

We find this intermediate love described in one of the most powerful and beautiful passages of the New Testament. This characterization of love has brought hope and comfort to half the world for nearly two thousand years. And it, too, was born as an ideal among a community of seekers who are here being advised to work with each other in a special way, to struggle with their emotional reactions in a special way. Although the word *agape* is used here, it is made to apply not so much to God's love for man, but to the love that men and women can work for in attending to each other's individual needs and strivings. To indicate the specific quality of this love, the King James Bible has rendered the word *agape* as *charity*, which in the ancient Latin translation is the term *caritas*. In the fourth century, through the thought of St. Augustine, the idea of a power of human love that brings together passion and impersonal love—*eros* and *agape*—was introduced through his interpretation of the word *caritas*. *Caritas* is the love that desires God, *a love which, directed to another human being, desires God for one's neighbor*. *Caritas*, translated as *charity* in the King James Bible, has little to do with philanthropy. It is more helpful, therefore, to render this word as *love* in these passages from the first letter of St. Paul to the Corinthians:

Though I speak with the tongues of men and of angels, and have not love, I am become as sounding brass, or a tinkling cymbal.

And though I have the gift of prophecy, and understand all mysteries, and all knowledge; and though I have all faith, so that I could remove mountains, and have not love, I am nothing.

And though I bestow all my goods to feed the poor, and though I give my body to be burned, and have not love, it profiteth me nothing.

Love suffereth long, and is kind; love envieth not; love vaunteth not itself, is not puffed up,

Doth not behave itself unseemly, seeketh not her own, is not easily provoked, thinketh no evil;

Rejoiceth not in iniquity, but rejoiceth in the truth;

Beareth all things, believeth all things, hopeth all things, endureth all things.

Love never faileth: but whether there be prophecies, they shall fail; whether there be tongues, they shall cease; whether there be knowledge, it shall vanish away.

For we know in part, and we prophesy in part.

But when that which is perfect is come, then that which is in part shall be done away.

When I was a child, I spake as a child, I understood as a child, I thought as a child: but when I became a man, I put away childish things.

For now we see through a glass, darkly; but then face to face: now I know in part; but then shall I know even as also I am known.

And now abideth faith, hope, love, these three; but the greatest of these is love.

(I Corinthians 13)

It is necessary to look more closely at these words of St. Paul. They can bring us the precise question we need to face in our lives together.

CONCLUSION
IN THE FORM OF
A QUESTION

We are here. The god of love has brought us here—in the midst of life with its cares and requirements, in the midst of time past and time future, here in our flawed and mortal bodies in which every small desire claims our attention. When we were falling in love, the intensity of our passion shielded us from the cares of life; when we were falling in love, time past and time future yielded their sovereignty to the fullness of the present moment; when we were falling in love, our bodies effortlessly submitted to the great universal forces pouring through them. Falling in love, even with all its anxiety and heartbreak, is received as a gift, a taste of another state of being. Nature gave us the gift of passion and in the reciprocity of passion with another, in presupposing always and in all things the other's passion for ourselves, we found a joyous intensity in which giving and receiving fused into one.

But now we are living together and something beyond passion is required of us. If we would work at love, it is no longer enough to presuppose the other's passion. Nature does not give a permanence of passion in any individual human being, nor, for that matter, in any living thing. For a man or woman, something intentional is required, an intentional work of love that carries through all the waves of passion and care and fear and distraction and forgetting, something intentional that carries through the periods of forgetting each other, the periods of temptation and imagination and the natural automatic attraction to new passion.

We cannot love as God loves or as a saint loves.

Nor, if we read the sacred texts right, does wisdom demand that of us. The love that St. Paul speaks of, the love that "builds up," that is long-suffering, free of envy and egoism, that does not seek personal gain and is not easily provoked and thinks no evil thoughts of the other—that love exists in us at the moment and for as long as an individual regards the other as seeking the truth, as harboring within him- or herself what the Buddhists call "the holy wish."

The work of love is the work of presupposing the wish for awakening in the other. In the midst of all that two people must face and live through together, the work of love silently acknowledges in the other the wish to become free from illusion, fear, egoism, false imagination, self-deception, tension, and violence; free from the power of life itself to devour our inner possibilities. The work of love, intermediate love, presupposes not only the wish to be free *from* these perennial weaknesses of the human condition—but to be free *for* contact with another quality of being in oneself, a conscious energy that is meant to penetrate the mind, heart, and body of every human being.

No human being can put this wish or this

search in another. But the beginning of intentional love is to assume its presence in the other and to return again and again to this unspoken assumption in the give-and-take of shared life. Understood in this way, the familiar words of St. Paul* have a new relevance for our present era. Understood in this way, Paul's vision of love can be approached as a parabolic mirror, gathering traces of the world's wisdom about love and directing it down toward the life of ordinary people struggling to love each other in a world that—as is perhaps the intrinsic nature of the world—is continually losing its heart and its soul.

Love suffereth long, and is kind. The work of love is to step back from the requirements we automatically place upon the other. When we assume that others are searching for themselves, we know that they are struggling to see their own weaknesses and betray-

---

* In the nineteenth century, the genius of Kierkegaard took these words of Paul and showed the modern world their practical existential meaning. For Kierkegaard the work of love was to assume love in the other. On this basis, the whole of the world's spiritual wisdom about love takes on new meaning. What we are speaking of here is a modest and fragmentary application of Kierkegaard's vision to the needs and subjectivity of our time and place.

als. Certainly there are mutual obligations between people, but *love cannot oblige another to be inwardly free.* Love assumes that the other, in the silence of self-confrontation, suffers from his or her own failures of will and attention. Love assumes the other wishes to see himself or herself even more clearly than we see him or her. The work of love is therefore to presuppose the wish for self-knowledge in the other.

But, as for kindness, this does not mean we do not respond, perhaps sometimes even with intensity, to painful words and acts. It is only that behind our own responses and reactions there remains the wish for the other's inner struggle. Even as one manifests anger or hurt, in the back of the psyche, underneath the anger or hurt, the work of love is to remember who we are and why we are on earth at all. In this dual state—in which one reacts and at the same time tries to remember the common search—it is possible to be angry without condemnation of the other's being, it is possible to be hurt without judging the other's heart and will. It goes without saying that to maintain this dual state in the midst of emotional reactions is very difficult. *But it is possible.*

• • •

Love . . . seeketh not her own. Obviously, much of what we ordinarily call love exists in the form of a bargain and obeys laws not unlike the laws of commerce. I will love you as long as you love me. I will care for you as long as you care for me. Or I will love you as long as what you do or who you are brings me something that I want. It would be foolish to pretend that human love can be free of this motivation. And why should it be? The whole of the natural world exists on the basis of reciprocal help and exchange. Nothing exists that does not serve, and nothing—no stone, plant, or animal—continues to exist without serving, without giving what is needed from it. Symbiosis in the broad sense is the law of nature. Interdependence is the law of nature.

Yet, love "seeketh not her own." Love seeks that the other can work for his or her own truth, which means—in the light of wisdom—his or her own *independent being*. Interdependence is the law of nature, yet the aim of human life is independent being, that is, being that is independent of the claims of the mortal body and the ephemeral, socially created self. For the human being, so wisdom teaches, independence means obedience to the permanent reality within and above ourselves. In the words of Kierkegaard: "love is essentially sacrifice. . . . For when a human being seeks the love of another human being, he seeks to become loved himself; this is not sacrifice; *sacrifice would consist precisely in helping the other person to seek God.*" (*Works of Love,* p. 247)

If interdependence is the law of life, we are here speaking of not so much another law but another kind of life and another kind of interdependence. When I help you, without any care for myself, only then am I helped. Fairy tales and legends, those which come from the heart of the world's wisdom teachings, continually speak to us of a reward that comes to men and women only if they seek no reward. The moment the thought of reward enters, the actions of love become part of another level of life—perhaps good and necessary on its own, but not the level of life that reflects the eternal in human nature. The fundamental mystery of all fairy tales and legends and, of course, the fundamental mystery of the Western world's defining *mythos* is the paradox of sacrificial love, love that "seeketh not her own." To assume the search in another is to become for a moment free of much that stands in the way of one's own inner search for meaning. To assume the search in another is to make room, mysteriously, for the truth to be experienced in oneself. The work of love is to struggle in oneself to adopt this assumption about the other at the very moment when all one's "natural impulses" of self-interest, healthy or otherwise, are pulling one toward psychological safety. Again, it is very difficult, *but it is possible.*

Love is not easily provoked, thinketh no evil. In fact, of course, most of us *are* easily provoked and we do think evil of the other, if by "evil" we include attributing to the other selfish and thoughtless motives. It is no wonder that these words of wisdom may seem a tiresome and hypocritical exhortation for us to behave like saints. Yet with these words, which seem so unrealistic, the teachings of wisdom actually indicate something essential about presupposing that the other is searching. The point is that this attitude toward the other needs to be more than a passing thought which we entertain while our emotional reactions go their own way. To assume the search in another may begin solely as a fascinating and hopeful new idea about how to regard other human beings. But, in actual fact, we cannot really assume that the other is searching unless we ourselves in that moment are seriously trying to attend to our own minds and hearts. To assume the search in another depends upon and, in turn, ignites the search in oneself, and, to some extent, frees us for a moment from the sway of fear and egoism. It is tiresome and hypocritical to demand of people that they experience no negative thoughts about the other. But what is new and hopeful about intermediate love is that the work of loving, without making us pretend to be saints, actually results in a taste of our own freedom from the egoistic emotions.

The miracle here or, if one wishes, the laws of the search are such that the act of seriously examining oneself without trying to improve anything at all actually results in the experience of freedom. Corresponding to this, the attempt to regard others as searching for themselves brings a return, at another level, of warmth toward the other that had disappeared under the sway of the emotional reactions. And, finally, this work of love toward the other sooner or later inevitably evokes the same kind of love *from* the other.

The legends of antiquity never let us forget that we have been born and that we will die. No matter what we do, no matter what drama, what absurdity, what triumph or defeat, what honor or nobility; no matter who acts or who is acted upon, who suffers or betrays, who helps or who hinders; no matter the glory or the shame; no matter the violence or the tenderness, or the wisdom or the stupidity— always and everywhere we are spoken of as "mortals," as beings who have been born and who will die. In this the legends of antiquity reflect the fundamental question of every human being who steps back from the vortex of life and asks and ponders the question of why we are here and what we are supposed to be.

To ask this question, not just intellectually but with the whole of one's being, is an intrinsic aspect of human nature. And, in the last analysis, it is a question that no one else can answer for us. Yet alongside the urgency and essential solitariness of the question of our life and our death, there exists the fact of love, its heat and warmth and the hope it can offer us. Alongside the essential aloneness of the question of why we live and die, there exists the communion of love. Love also is an intrinsic defining aspect of human nature and human life.

Somewhere, somehow, the power of love seems to offer itself as an answer to the painful riddle of death. Yet the legends of antiquity and our own human experience often show us that love ultimately fails to answer that riddle. Although the joy and suffering of the love that is given us take us again and again to the threshold of an answer, again and again we are delivered back to the finite time-driven sense of self that we know is mortal and weak and, it may seem, ultimately meaningless.

The question then arises: Do we love with an intensity and power that is equal to the fact of our mortality? We are not gods; we are men and women. We are called "mortals." That is, our mortality defines us.

Or does it? Again the question: Do we love with the quality and the power that is possible for us? Death is given to us, we cannot escape it. But is the love that is given to us meant to be the answer to the finitude that brings us to question who and what we are? Love is surely the answer to death. But what kind of love? And how do we find it?

Throughout the ages, in every period of history, specific teachings and practices have been offered to mankind that point to the possibility of transcending our seemingly inescapable finitude. These teachings may be likened to gods visiting among the mortals—Jupiter in all his far-reaching power, and Mercury, whose role is, by any and all means, to further communication between the gods and mortals. Jupiter is the ruler of the eternally real; Mercury speaks of it to human beings and shows them the way: *if they wish for it.*

Essential to all such teachings is that the way to the new life cannot be forced upon human beings, either through fear or seduction or logic that compels only the mind, or through habit and blind obedience. The gifts that come from the gods must be asked for, freely, from oneself alone. Countless are the legends and tales that speak of the paramount importance of knowing what to wish for, and of the tragedy that awaits men and women who wish foolishly or egoistically.

Do these gods, these teachings, still walk the earth? What kind of garments are they wearing?

The story of Baucis and Philemon may be taken as a symbolic hint of the kind of love that can develop between two people who are searching for truth and who wish to serve the truth. Perhaps it is that kind of love, as it blends with the mortal joys and needs of our lives together, which leads men and women beyond their finitude. We may then say, without a trace of sentimentality or wishful thinking, that love is stronger than death. In the words of St. Paul: "Love abides."

FOR FURTHER READING

Coleman Barks with John Moyne, *The Essential Rumi*. San Francisco: HarperSanFrancisco, 1985. Gathers into one volume all the extraordinary new renditions of Rumi by the American poet Coleman Barks.

Bhagavad Gita, translated by Eknath Easwaran. Petaluma, California: Nilgiri Press, 1985. One of the best modern translations of this timeless classic of Indian spirituality.

Erich Fromm, *The Art of Loving*. New York: Harper & Row, 1989. A modern classic of psychological analysis that has influenced and helped generations of men and women.

G. I. Gurdjieff, *Views from the Real World*. New York: Arkana, 1984. The chapters "The Three Powers" and "There Are Two Kinds of Love" offer a glimpse of the great teacher's understanding of conscious love.

Søren Kierkegaard, *Works of Love*, translated by Howard and Edna Hong. New York: Harper Torchbooks, 1962. Possibly the most profound study of the subject in modern literature.

J. Krishnamurti, *Freedom from the Known*. New York: Harper & Row, 1969. The chapter on love is beautiful, challenging, and original.

Thomas Merton, *Love and Living*. New York: Harcourt, Brace and Jovanovich, 1979. A dynamic and profound Christian discourse on love.

Anders Nygren, *Agape and Eros*. New York: Harper & Row, 1969. A magnificent, pioneering study of the Christian idea of love.

A. R. Orage, *On Love*. New York: Samuel Weiser, 1974. The celebrated English critic and pupil of Gurdjieff offers a penetrating and lucid exposition of the idea of conscious love.

P. D. Ouspensky, *Tertium Organum*. New York: Alfred A. Knopf, 1981. A breathtaking, synoptic work of metaphysical philosophy. The chapters on the emotions and on love are truly visionary.

Plato, *The Symposium*. One of the most influential treatises on love in the history of the west, and one of the most beautiful and powerful of Plato's dialogues.

Rilke on Love and Other Difficulties, translated by John J. L. Mood. New York: W. W. Norton, 1975, pp. 25–35. Nowhere is the subject of love treated with such a blending of compassion and realism.

Denis de Rougemont, *Love in the Western World.* New York: Pantheon Books, Inc., 1956. A brilliant and startling critique of love in the history of Western civilization.